D0848642

# Changing Education

## ALTERNATIVES
## FROM
## EDUCATIONAL RESEARCH

PRENTICE-HALL AMERICAN EDUCATIONAL
RESEARCH ASSOCIATION SERIES

*Research in Teacher Education:*
*A Symposium*
B. Othanel Smith

*Changing Education:*
*Alternatives From Educational Research*
M. C. Wittrock

## CONTRIBUTORS

Richard C. Atkinson, *Stanford University*

James S. Coleman, *Johns Hopkins University*

Robert Glaser, *University of Pittsburgh*

Evan R. Keislar, *University of California, Los Angeles*

William D. Rohwer, Jr., *University of California, Berkeley*

Michael Scriven, *University of California, Berkeley*

Alberta E. Siegel, *Stanford University Medical Center*

Patrick Suppes, *Stanford University*

M. C. Wittrock, *University of California, Los Angeles*

# Changing Education

## ALTERNATIVES
## FROM
## EDUCATIONAL RESEARCH

*Edited by*

M. C. WITTROCK

*University of California, Los Angeles*

*for the American Educational
Research Association*

PRENTICE-HALL, INC., *Englewood Cliffs, N.J.*

Library of Congress Cataloging in Publication Data
Main entry under title.

Changing education: alternatives from educational
research.

Eight invited addresses given at the 1972 AERA annual
convention.
Includes bibliographical references.
1. Educational research—Addresses, essays, lectures.
2. Teaching—Addresses, essays, lectures.   I. Wittrock,
Merlin C., ed.   II. Atkinson, Richard C.   III. American
Educational Research Association.
LB1028.C48        370′.78′073        73-1892
ISBN   0-13-128256-5

10   9   8   7   6   5   4   3   2   1

*Printed in the United States of America*

PRENTICE-HALL INTERNATIONAL, INC., London
PRENTICE-HALL OF AUSTRALIA PTY. LTD., Sydney
PRENTICE-HALL OF CANADA LTD., Toronto
PRENTICE-HALL OF INDIA PRIVATE LIMITED, New Delhi
PRENTICE-HALL OF JAPAN, INC., Tokyo

# Contents

# I

## THE RELEVANCE OF RESEARCH TO IMPROVING EDUCATION

# 1

v

# II

## ALTERNATIVE CONCEPTIONS OF EDUCATIONAL RESEARCH

# III

## ALTERNATIVE DIRECTIONS FOR RESEARCH IN INSTRUCTION AND TEACHING

# IV

## NEW DIRECTIONS IN SCHOOLING

# ❧ I ❧

# THE RELEVANCE OF RESEARCH TO IMPROVING EDUCATION

# The Need for
# Research-based Alternatives

## M. C. WITTROCK

## THE ORIGIN OF THE VOLUME

This volume reports the texts of eight invited addresses given at the 1972 AERA Annual Convention. The theme of the volume, "Alternatives from Educational Research," was a main theme of the 1972 Annual Meeting of the American Educational Research Association. All four of the association sponsored addresses delivered at the meeting were designed to contribute to the development of the theme. These addresses were delivered by Richard C. Atkinson, James S. Coleman, Michael Scriven, and Alberta Siegel. In addition, four other invited addresses given at the 1972 AERA Annual Meeting directly pertained to the theme. These addresses were given by Robert Glaser, Evan Keislar, William Rohwer, Jr., and Patrick Suppes. The present volume consists of these eight invited addresses, which present research-based alternatives relevant for changing schools, for modifying the directions of educational research, and for changing the theoretical conceptions of education, especially the theoretical conceptions of learning and instruction.

The volume and its theme arose in the following way. An important part of my duties as Program Chairman of the 1972 AERA Annual Meeting was to select and to invite the speakers to deliver the association sponsored addresses. Another responsibility of mine was to design a volume which would be published as the second one in the AERA–Prentice-Hall

Series, which is designed to report the results of a session or of a set of sessions occurring at the AERA Annual Meetings.*

From these two responsibilities came the decision to organize the association-sponsored invited addresses and the AERA–Prentice-Hall volume around a theme that is important to a large number of educational researchers. Alternatives *from* educational research was chosen as the theme for invited addresses and for this volume. The reasons for this choice are discussed below.

## THE REASONS FOR THE THEME

The primary reason for choosing "Alternatives from Educational Research" as the theme of this volume is that educational researchers are continually developing, but not often widely communicating, their research-based alternatives for changing schooling, for understanding learning and teaching, and for modifying educational research programs. In recent years, many of the most widely discussed alternative conceptualizations of education have not been based upon empirical research, nor have they been associated with the names of empirical researchers.

One reason for the limited attention sometimes given to research-based alternatives in education is indigenous to the methods of reporting scientific research. The limitations, constraints, and caveats that must accompany conscientiously prepared reports of educational research sometimes dampen popular enthusiasm for research-based alternatives.

It is often difficult to motivate educators or researchers to action through written reports detailing the results, import, and limitations of research. These communications are usually written in tenuous, guarded styles consistent with the canons of reporting research. As a result, with readers facing important, concrete problems of teaching, it is difficult for reports of educational research to compete successfully with the often persuasively written, non-research based articles and books. The authors of these latter books and articles have a significant advantage and freedom not shared by educational researchers. These authors who are not researchers are not constrained to determine empirically before propounding them the uses and limitations of their ideas.

In sum, then, the first and primary reason for selection of the theme of this volume is to remind us that, in its own deliberate way, educational research offers selected, tested alternatives for change in education. The

* The first volume in the AERA–Prentice-Hall series is entitled *Research in Teacher Education*. Edited by B. Othanel Smith and published in 1971, the volume reports the proceedings of a symposium held at the 1970 AERA Annual Meeting.

book should help emphasize that, by its nature, educational research is a quest for alternatives, for change, for new ways to solve old problems.

The second reason for selecting the theme of this volume is to give several examples of how research-based alternatives are distinctive and different from non-research based alternatives. Research involves methodological safeguards that proscribe untested innovations and ideas. There are strict rules to be followed by researchers who would suggest change and alternatives. The ideas and generalizations of researchers must be subjected to replicable, empirical tests or studies before they can have scientific credence and respectability.

Not everyone who wants to find new and better solutions to the problems of education is willing to subject his ideas to carefully designed empirical tests and to live with their consequences. These consequences might include discovering that one's ideas were limited in utility, not important, perhaps trivial. Not everyone interested in changing education is willing to accept this risk of failure, or to wait the years required to build a successful, research-based alternative useful for solving a significant problem in education.

Not everyone should accept the researcher's credo and methods. To create new solutions to the problems of education, we need both the empirically tested generalizations of the researcher and the non-researcher's sage insights.

The reasons then for publishing this volume are (1) to ensure that at least several research-based alternatives for education are given increased attention to help to balance the heavy attention given today to non-research based alternatives and, (2) to emphasize the distinctiveness of research-based alternatives to education.

## ❧ 1 ❧

# Facts and Fantasies
# of Education

## PATRICK SUPPES

The text for my sermon today is the closing paragraph of Hume's *Enquiries Concerning Human Understanding.*

> When we run over libraries, persuaded of these principles [Hume's principles of the understanding], what havoc must we make? If we take in our hand any volume; of divinity or school metaphysics, for instance; let us ask, *Does it contain any abstract reasoning concerning quantity or number?* No. *Does it contain any experimental reasoning concerning matter of fact and existence?* No. Commit it then to the flames: for it can contain nothing but sophistry and illusion.

Hume would be the first to admit that we are all entitled to our fantasies, but he would also insist that we recognize them as the fantasies they are. To reformulate his text, general ideas about educational policy and practice contain little but sophistry and illusion, unless they can be defended by abstract reasoning from some other accepted general principles or be inferred in a definite manner from particular matters of fact.

This sounds like a hard line, and it is. It is too hard to be used at all times and places in discussions of educational policy and practice, but it

Patrick Suppes, "Facts and Fantasies of Education." This address, originally written for the AERA, is also reprinted with permission of Phi Delta Kappa, Incorporated.

is not too hard for a reflective occasion like this one, which is aimed at appraising the relevance of research to educational ideas.

Rather than begin with any general remarks or general propositions, I shall first report some of the results of perusing my own library and applying Hume's tests. The initial examples that I critically examine will be those that most of us can sagely and benignly agree about. I shall move on to others that are more controversial and, for that reason, probably more important.

Rewording Hume's text still once again, the thesis of this paper may be expressed succinctly in the following way: Without proper evidence, alleged facts on which educational policy or practice is based can only be classed as fantasies. It is the task of research to convert the "right" fantasies into facts and to show the others to be the unsubstantial fantasies they are.

Before turning to particular examples, I want to say a preliminary word about evidence. I have a somewhat skeptical and Bayesian attitude. I do not think it is possible to state in mathematically precise terms what is to count as evidence and what is not. Evidence also need not be collected by systematic experimentation. The most glorious quantitative science of them all, namely, astronomy, has scarcely ever been able to include experiments. Evidence is also not just a matter of quantitative data, organized in obvious quantitative fashion. We do not need to perform an experiment or take systematic observations in order to hold the firm factual belief that the sun will rise tomorrow. On the other hand, when we turn to the formulation of general principles or general ideas about human conduct and how that conduct might be changed by the process of education, we must forever be wary and skeptical of those who promise much in general terms and give us principles unsupported by evidence.

I fully recognize also that over large periods of time most people are indeed taken in by some unsupported principles. One of the most sobering facts I know is that one of the earliest English charities was organized to collect money to buy wood to burn witches. The record of human folly committed in the name of morality or truth is too long and dismal to survey here.

At this point, I turn to some examples that give a more vivid sense of the continued need and the vital place of research in education. I consider initially what I call "first-order fantasies." These are fantasies about general ways of organizing education in matters of theory, policy or practice. Afterward I turn to "second-order fantasies," which are fantasies about methodology or about how we should determine the truth or falsity of first-order fantasies. Remember that in the sense I am using the terms here, fantasies of either the first or second order can be good fantasies in the sense that they can be true. It is the task of research to produce the evidence that will convert them from fantasies to fact.

## FIRST-ORDER FANTASIES

I begin with a classic example of applied linguistics.

### Linguistic Fantasies about Reading

The importance and significance of the work of the American linguist Leonard Bloomfield is widely recognized and not challenged by me. The very quality of Bloomfield as a linguist makes all the more striking the simplicity of his ideas and his apparent total unawareness of the need for data in recommending how reading should be taught. His ideas are set forth in the book *Let's Read, A Linguistic Approach* (1961), jointly authored with Clarence L. Barnhart and published some years after Bloomfield's death.

So as not to enter into too elaborate an analysis, I shall restrict myself to Bloomfield's recommendations about the first materials of reading. He enunciates in a few paragraphs (pp. 39–42) the following:

1. "Our first material must show each letter in only one phonetic value."
2. "Our first material should contain no words with silent letters (such as *knit* or *gnat*) and none with double letters, and none with combinations of letters having a special value (as *th* in *then* or *be* in *bean*)."
3. "The letter *x* cannot be used, because it represents two phonemes (*ks* or *gz*)."
4. "The letter *q* cannot be used, because it occurs only in connection with an unusual value of the letter *u*."
5. "The best selection of values of letters to be used in the first materials for reading is the following," and here follows a large set of recommendations.
6. "Our first reading materials will consist of two-letter and three-letter words in which the letters have the sound values given in the above list."
7. "We should not, at this stage, ask the child to write or print the words: that comes much later."
8. "The early reading lessons should not be very long, for they demand a severe intellectual effort. It may be well to take up only two words in the first lesson."
9. "In the second lesson, after review, add two or three more words of the same group."

10. "The drill should continue until the child can read correctly any one of the words when the parent or teacher points to it."

11. "If the child has learned the pattern in the list of actual words, he should be able to read nonsense syllables using the same pattern. . . . The nonsense syllables are a test of the child's mastery of the phoneme. Tell the child the nonsense syllables are parts of real words which he will find in the books that he reads."

12. "The acquisition of nonsense syllables is an important part of the task of mastering the reading process. The child will learn the patterns of the language more rapidly if you use the nonsense syllables in teaching." [1]

A number of additional principles (pp. 19–42) are stated, but I have given a large enough sample to indicate in an explicit way why I label these principles *Bloomfield's fantasies*. They represent one of the purest examples of an analysis of one kind being extrapolated and applied to a different kind of problem without recognition of the need for data and for evaluation of the correctness of principles in their new application. Bloomfield applies some fairly obvious phonetic principles and generalizations, but shows no recognition at any point of the need for data to check on the correctness of these principles as principles of reading.

As I use *fantasy* here, a fantasy can be correct or true, but it remains a fantasy unless proper evidence is offered, and this is certainly the case for what Bloomfield offers us for principles about reading. It is almost breathtaking to have him assert, for example, the principle that children learn language more rapidly if nonsense syllables are used in teaching. To fail to recognize the need for data and to state such a learning principle without any systematic concept of learning seems, in our currently skeptical time, almost incredible.

### Piaget's Stages

The influence of Jean Piaget on developmental psychology is recognized throughout the world. His very status, however, as an imaginative creator of new concepts and theories about children's behavior and development has led to an often uncritical acceptance of his ideas. I select for emphasis in the present discussion his concept of stages of development, which has played such a central part in many of his works and has also been taken over into developmental psycholinguistics. At first glance one might think that the concept of stages of development is a methodologically innocent one and scarcely a subject of controversy. A perusal of Piaget's own writings and the

[1] From *Let's Read, A Linguistic Approach*, by L. Bloomfield and C. L. Barnhart (Detroit, Mich.: Wayne State University Press, 1961). Reprinted by permission.

large derivative corpus soon leads one to another conclusion. As an example I shall discuss the analysis of three stages of multiple seriation in *The Early Growth of Logic in the Child* by Bärbel Inhelder and Piaget (1964).

To indicate the unequivocal adoption of the idea of stages, I quote from page 270:

> We shall distinguish three stages, corresponding to the usual three levels. During stage I, there are no seriations in the strict sense. The child's constructions are intermediate between classification and seriation. . . . During stage II, there is seriation, but only according to one of the criteria, or else the child switches from one criterion to the other. . . . Finally, during stage III (starting at 7–8 years), the child reaches a multiplicative arrangement based on the twofold seriation of the set of elements.

There is in this discussion, as elsewhere in Piaget, no suggestion that matters could be otherwise—that development could be incremental and continuous and that no stages could be identified in nonconventional fashion. To adopt the idea of stages as a convenient, conventional way of talking in certain restricted contexts is, of course, quite natural.[2] It is another thing to talk as if they were real abstractions with a verifiable and unequivocal empirical content.

It is a truism that children develop new capacities and new skills as they get older. The problem in evaluating the existence of stages is not one of affirming this truism, but rather one of differentiating the concept of stages from the equally natural concept of continuous development.

A second related problem that needs detailed study is the extent to which the mastery of different concepts follows the same order in different children. Again, it is important that the experimental design be as meticulous as possible in order not to prejudge the issue. It can scarcely be said that Piaget's design in the study I am considering satisfies this criterion, and very few others of like nature do either.

Moreover, if nonconventional plateaus were discovered in the behavior of individual children, we would also want to know whether these plateaus run across the same set of concepts or occur in a manner that is much more randomly related to the concepts themselves and that might reflect quite different sorts of processes of maturation in the child. Again, little evidence is to be found on this point.

My first draft of these remarks on the concept of stages received an excellent critique from Harry Beilin, and he has provided me references to

---

[2] Roger Brown puts the matter nicely: ". . . one naturally falls into the habit of speaking of stage I and stage II and so on. There is no harm in that so long as we recognize that these are imposed stages, laid upon continuous data by the investigator as an analytic convenience [*Psycholinguistics*, 1970, p. 100]."

his own work and that of Piaget where the question of the actual existence of stages is discussed. Piaget writes:

> I now come to the big problem: the problem of the very existence of stages; do there exist steps in development or is complete continuity observed? . . . [W]hen we are faced macroscopically with a certain discontinuity we never know whether there do not exist small transformations which would be continuous but which we do not manage to measure on our scale of approximation. In other words, continuity would depend fundamentally on a question of scale; for a certain scale of measurement we obtain discontinuity when with a finer scale we should get continuity. Of course this argument is quite valid, because the very manner of defining continuity and discontinuity implies that these ideas remain fundamentally relative to the scale of measurement or observation. This, then, is the alternative which confronts us: either a basic continuity or else development by steps, which would allow us to speak of stages at least to our scale of approximation [1960, p. 121].

A more detailed and careful analytical discussion of the concept of stages is to be found in Beilin (1971), and he raises a number of issues that are not pertinent to the main point I wish to make here. In the printed discussion following Beilin's paper, there are remarks by Piaget that seem to me incorrect and, in general, incorrect for the same reasons that the above quotation about the existence of stages is incorrect. In the context of Beilin's paper Piaget (1971, p. 194) is discussing the problem of novelty, and he has this to say:

> Thus, to my regret, I did not find in Beilin's paper any reference to this problem of novelty—of the formation of novelties in general and the conditions necessary for the development of new structure. . . . If there are no novelties, then the concept of stages is artificial. There lies the whole problem.

Before commenting directly on these remarks of Piaget's, I want to compare the almost total absence of serious critical analysis of the concept of stages with the controversy in learning theory that existed about ten years ago between all-or-none and incremental learning. In the latter case the battle was joined with intensity and fruitful result because there were strong protagonists on both sides of the argument, and each was determined to establish the incorrectness of the other's view and, if possible, the correctness of his own view. A large number of experiments were performed, and quite detailed analyses were made of the data to test whether or not the learning of simple concepts or simple associations satisfied all-or-none or incremental properties. Analyses with special relevance to concept formation in children are to be found in Suppes (1965) and Suppes and Ginsburg (1963). For the purpose of this discussion, the all-or-none model would correspond to Piaget's idea of stages, and the tests of incremental learning models to the continuous learning that is the natural alternative to stages. We need the kind of sharp exchange and critical examination of experiments and concepts characteristic of that learning-theoretic controversy of a decade ago in the analysis of the concept of stages in developmental psychology.

It should be apparent that the attitudes expressed in the quotations from Piaget do not provide the basis for this kind of sharp exchange and critical examination. Piaget raises what is essentially an irrelevant question of scale. The problem is to find out for the *given* scale at which experimentation is conducted whether the process is all-or-none or incremental, and not whether there are microscales, for example, at which the process is continuous even if the data indicate all-or-none learning at the ordinary scale of experimentation. The second remark about novelty also seems to me to miss the point, especially as reflected in the extensive work on all-or-none learning in concept identification as opposed to concept formation experiments. It certainly is perfectly possible that learning is all-or-none or in terms of stages even when no questions of novelty are involved. There is also no reason to think that when concept formation and mastery of novel concepts are evident that learning is necessarily to be characterized in terms of stages rather than incrementally. I say once again that the element missing in this discussion by Piaget, and even by Beilin in his otherwise excellent article, is the concept of precise and detailed experimentation with quantitative analysis of data to test for the existence of stages.

Finding out the true state of affairs about stages is important not simply for theoretical purposes in developmental psychology, but because continual use of these concepts is found in the talk of educators in their organization of curriculum for young children, in their discussion of the skills of young children, and in other related ways. It would be easy to document the continual casual reference to Piaget in a variety of educational publications in which teachers are once again being taught dogma without data that developmental stages are the way to think about the development of children.

I cannot resist one passing remark on this matter of stages and concepts like that of groupement and seriation. The very language used by Piaget and his more ardent followers is itself a kind of fantasy of mathematics. Those of good faith can believe that back of such talk is a real body of concepts that can be put into reasonable order. Those of us who are more skeptical face the beginning of the fantasies here and wait for a new round of theory and experiments to clear the air.

A comparative point of intellectual history is perhaps in order. There is much about Piaget's ideas that resembles the kind of suggestive web woven by Descartes in his principles of philosophy. Descartes, of course, was dealing with the physical world and Piaget with the psychological world of child development. Both operate in large theoretical terms and with little regard for detailed experimental investigation. Descartes' tale proved to be enormously seductive in the seventeenth century, and even Newton found it difficult to throw off the Cartesian ideas. Leibnitz, however, put it correctly when he characterized Descartes' physics as a *roman de physique,* and I shall be bold enough to say that we may very likely in the future characterize Piaget's work as a *roman de psychologie.* To say this is not to deny that Descartes has occupied an important place in the history of physics or that Piaget has occupied an important place in the history of psychology. It is rather to put in proper perspective large-scale theories that are as close to fantasies as they are to facts.

## Skinner on Arithmetic

As an example of a different sort, but at the same first-order level of fantasy, I next would like to consider what Skinner has to say about teaching arithmetic in his book *The Technology of Teaching* (1968, pp. 14–15). Here is the opening passage on arithmetic.

> From this exciting prospect of an advancing science of learning, it is a great shock to turn to that branch of technology which is most directly concerned with the learning process—education. Let us consider, for example, the teaching of arithmetic in the lower grades. The school is concerned with imparting to the child a large number of responses of a special sort. The responses are all verbal. They consist of speaking and writing certain words, figures, and signs which, to put it roughly, refer to numbers and to arithmetic operations. The first task is to shape these responses—to get the child to pronounce and to write responses correctly, but the principal task is to bring this behavior under many sorts of stimulus control. This is what happens when the child learns to count, to recite tables, to count while ticking off the items in an assemblage of objects, to respond to spoken or written numbers by saying "odd," "even," or "prime." Over and above this elaborate repertoire of numerical behavior, most of which is often dismissed as the product of rote learning, the teaching of arithmetic looks forward to those complex serial arrangements of responses involved in original mathematical thinking. The child must acquire responses of transposing, clearing fractions, and so on, which modify the order or pattern of the original material so that the response called a solution is eventually made possible.

The crudeness of this talk about responses and shaping them without serious reference to how arithmetical concepts should be built up is typical of this strange and undocumented proposal of how arithmetic ought to be taught. The naive and impressionistic character of the remarks is attested to by the juxtaposition of the words "odd," "even," and "prime" in the middle of the passage. The very special role, for example, of students' ever responding *prime* to spoken or written numbers is to be emphasized. The casual way of talking about moving from arithmetic to "those complex serial arrangements of responses involved in original mathematical thinking" is a reflection of how vague and unsubstantial Skinners' ideas about the teaching of arithmetic or other parts of mathematics are. It would be interesting indeed to have those complex serial arrangements of responses made to match any serious piece of mathematical instruction, let alone original mathematical thinking. The casual talk about acquiring "responses of transposing, clearing fractions, and so on" is again indicative of the unthought-out and undocumented character of the remarks.

No evidence is offered about the effectiveness of these ideas for the teaching of arithmetic. What is more important—it would not even be clear from this passage or the passages that follow how any teacher would begin to arrange the complex material of arithmetic in proper order for learning by children. It would be interesting to see what Skinner would have to say about the detailed sequence of materials in arithmetic, and how the proper arrangement of materials should be made, according to which principles and on the basis of what data. It is especially ironic to have such a broad and unsubstantiated sketch of how arithmetic should be taught without reference to any of the extensive literature on the learning of arithmetic.

I cannot think of a better challenge to Skinnerians than to produce a genuine psychological theory of mathematical learning and thinking. So far as I know, there is not yet a serious contribution from either Skinner or his followers on this important educational topic. In some quarters at least, I am sure the fantasy will remain that somehow operant conditioning is the key to successful mathematical learning.

## SECOND-ORDER FANTASIES

By a second-order fantasy I mean a belief about the efficacy or lack of it of a certain methodology, which is unsupported by evidence or systematic argument. I begin with an example much closer to home than any I have yet considered and refer to the writings of two authors with whom I am in general intellectually sympathetic.

### Campbell and Stanley on Experimentation

The fantasy I have in mind is the unsupported and yet wholly enthusiastic support of experimentation by Campbell and Stanley in their well-known chapter on this subject in the *Handbook of Research on Teaching* (1963). As most of you will remember, the handbook was itself a product of AERA. Let me begin with two quotations from the second and third pages of the chapter.

> This chapter is committed to the experiment: as the only means for settling disputes regarding educational practice, as the only way of verifying educational improvements, and as the only way of establishing a cumulative tradition in which improvements can be introduced without the danger of a faddish discard of old wisdom in favor of inferior novelties. . . . [E]ven though we recognize experimentation as the basic language of proof, as the only decision court for disagreement between rival theories, we should not expect that "crucial experiments" which pit opposing theories will be likely to have clear-cut outcomes. When one finds, for example, that competent observers advocate strongly divergent points of view, it seems likely on a priori grounds that both have observed something valid about the natural situation, and that both represent a part of the truth. The stronger the controversy, the more likely this is. Thus we might expect in such cases an experimental outcome with mixed results, or with the balance of truth varying subtly from experiment to experiment.

As matters of personal belief, I accept with certain reservations what Campbell and Stanley have to say in the quoted passages. What I am criticizing is the lack of argument for the position, and for this reason I have labeled the passage an example of a second-order fantasy. The chapter contains no systematic examination of alternatives to experimentation, no review of sciences like astronomy which do not engage in experimentation in any serious way and yet achieve remarkable results, no attempt to formulate general principles to make it clear why experimentation is so important; in fact, there is no scientifically serious attempt to define the concept of an experiment.

I emphasize that I do not have in mind a rigorous formal treatment of the concept of an experiment, but rather a densely argued informal consideration of the principles of evidence that offer a systematic defense of the use of experimental procedures. For example, within a Bayesian framework (I do not mean to suggest that they necessarily should adopt such a framework), one can argue that the likelihoods, as opposed to the prior distributions of opinion or belief, can be agreed upon by different investigators of different theoretical persuasions. It is the practical possibility of agreement on likelihood functions that makes experimentation attractive. We can of course go on to ask the deeper question, why is it that different individuals of quite different orientations can agree on likelihood functions and the conceptual scheme of experimentation when they are far apart theoretically? It is not always true that they can so agree, but it is true often enough that an analysis can be given of the reasons for agreement in a wide range of circumstances.

My own view would be that the defense should be built on the basis of the different status of different kinds of knowledge. We can, for instance, agree on how a given group of students answered the items on a test if the test was multiple choice, but we may not be able to agree on how to interpret the results, or if we gave an essay test how to evaluate even narrowly the essay responses. It seems to me that the defense of experimentation depends heavily on the drawing of such distinctions between the kinds of knowledge we have.

The second major aspect of classical psychological and educational experimentation centers around the difficult and elusive concept of randomization. Here too, it seems to me that Campbell and Stanley do not give the research worker in search of help a detailed and closely argued defense of the reasons for randomizing in experiments. If the authors felt that the subtle topic of randomization was too difficult a one to enter into, clear warnings should have been given the readers that they were not attempting any defense of the concept and that it was being taken on faith as a wonderful thing.

Later in the chapter there is a section entitled "Some Preliminary Comments on the Theory of Experimentation," and once again wise remarks are made about statistical lore and experimental practice. What is missing, however, is that sense of intellectual openness on the one hand and precision of argument on the other so very much required in the theory of experimentation, or, more generally, in applied statistics. Applying Hume's dichotomy of having either reasoning about abstract matters or evidence about matters of fact, we find that both the quotation given above and the longer section on the theory of experimentation are neither organized around abstract principles from which more principles of experimentation are derived, nor validated by a systematic collection of empirical evidence bearing on the theory of experimentation.

It is appropriate to add weight to these general statements by some more detailed examples. There are at least three respects in which I think the innocent reader might be misled by Campbell and Stanley's generally excellent article. To begin with, the deeper and more varied the contact a person has with applied statistics, the more evident it is that some experience in seeing the statistical procedures and tests of significance derived from first principles is of importance. It is too easy for the innocent researcher to divorce in his mind the simple algebraic formulation of particular tests or procedures from the probabilistic background that justifies their derivation and interpretation. I am not suggesting something that I think is easy to do within the restrictions Campbell and Stanley set for themselves; however, some sense of derivation from first principles in at least one example would deepen considerably the basis the reader would have for accepting the kinds of distinctions introduced.

My second remark is a more serious and important one. Already at the beginning of the nineteenth century, in his treatise on the theory of probability, Laplace (1820) emphasized the importance of not simply establishing the existence of an effect, but establishing a method for estimating the magnitude of an effect. From a broad methodological standpoint, perhaps the single most important criticism one might make of the statistical procedures used and exemplified in the *Journal of Experimental Psychology,* methods of which Campbell and Stanley in general approve, is the overwhelming use of tests of significance establishing the existence of effects, in contrast to the almost total absence of tests that estimate magnitudes of effects.

A simple, but powerful, analysis of such an example is provided by Laplace's attempt to estimate the benefits of inoculation for smallpox by variolar virus before vaccine was available. (Laplace concluded that the mean increased longevity from inoculation was about three years, provided that there was no food shortage or other violent disruption of the environment.) Such estimates of the magnitude of causal effects are of the first importance in both pure and applied science, and it is especially important to bring them more to the fore in educational research. We may leave to the psychologists aloft in the pages in the *Journal of Experimental Psychology* the design of experiments that test for *existence* of effects. In education we are much more concerned with estimating *magnitudes* of effects. If, for example, a new curriculum that costs twice as much as an old curriculum produces a measurable effect, but that measurable effect is very small in magnitude, then the practical use of this curriculum is questionable.

Mentioning the problem of estimating magnitudes of effects suggests immediately broadening the framework of statistical analysis to that of statistical decision theory. For many educational experiments, this would result in a three-fold decision procedure: accept the new procedure of instruction, reject it, or continue further experimentation where the current verdict of nothing yet proved would lead to a new look at experimental procedures, and especially their interpretation. But I shall not attempt to explore these matters further in the present context.

My third and final comment on the "interior analysis" of Campbell and Stanley's chapter concerns some remarks they make about linear models. In discussing tests of significance for time series designs, on page 43 they assert "Statistical tests would probably involve, in all but the most extended time series, linear fits to the data, both for convenience and because more exact fitting would exhaust the degrees of freedom, leaving no opportunity to test the hypothesis of change."

It seems to me that here is an example of simplifying too drastically and therefore introducing a small-scale kind of fantasy too easily adopted by educational researchers. It is a fantasy that we must always test for linear relations, because we have no ability to handle nonlinear ones. Especially with the use of modern computers, it is almost as easy to deal with simple nonlinear models as linear ones. Exploring the alternatives to linearity provides excellent insight into the nature of the relations between the variables and does not require necessarily the use of more degrees of freedom. Let us consider, for example, just the simple case of two variables, with $x$ the independent variable and $y$ the dependent variable. We may express the linear model by the following equation:

$$y = a + bx.$$

This model has two parameters to be estimated from the data and thus two degrees of freedom are lost. If we think of the effects of increase in $x$ on $y$ proceeding at a faster than linear fashion, we can estimate the same number of parameters for the quadratic model:

$$y = a + bx^2.$$

On the other hand, if we think of the nonlinear increase in $y$ with increases in $x$ as less than linear, we can easily test the logarithmic model:

$$y = a + b \log x.$$

There is much more to be said about these matters, and I am not pretending to give a detailed analysis to complement these brief remarks. It is just that in my search for fantasies I have tried to look everywhere, even among some of the best established and generally most sensible sources.

## Chomsky's Theory of Competence

As a second example of a second-order fantasy, I select Chomsky's theory of competence. If the ideas that he seems to be putting forth were correct, they would have some fairly far-reaching implications for educational research and educational practice. I classify his remarks quoted below as second order, because they recommend an approach to the study of behavior that is at considerable variance with current emphases. The following passage (*Language and Mind*, 1972, pp. 72–73) states Chomsky's methodological point in succinct form.

The theory of generative grammar, both particular and universal, points to a conceptual lacuna in psychological theory that I believe is worth mentioning. Psychology conceived as "behavioral science" has been concerned with behavior and acquisition or control of behavior. It has no concept corresponding to "competence," in the sense in which competence is characterized by a generative grammar. The theory of learning has limited itself to a narrow and surely inadequate concept of what is learned—namely a system of stimulus-response connections, a network of associations, a repertoire of behavioral items, a habit hierarchy, or a system of dispositions to respond in a particular way under specifiable stimulus conditions. Insofar as behavioral psychology has been applied to education or therapy, it has correspondingly limited itself to this concept of "what is learned." But a generative grammar cannot be characterized in these terms. What is necessary, in addition to the concept of behavior and learning, is a concept of what is learned—a notion of competence—that lies beyond the conceptual limits of behaviorist psychological theory. Like much of modern linguistics and modern philosophy of language, behaviorist psychology has quite consciously accepted methodological restrictions that do not permit the study of systems of the necessary complexity and abstractness. One important future contribution of the study of language to general psychology may be to focus attention on this conceptual gap and to demonstrate how it may be filled by the elaboration of a system of underlying competence in one domain of human intelligence.[3]

As in the case of Skinner, the thesis set forth by Chomsky is breathtaking in its dogmatic simplicity. It could be said that it seems dogmatically simple only because I am quoting the introduction of a long and complex empirical or theoretical argument. Substantial formal arguments and substantial empirical data are offered subsequently, and I have distorted the analysis by restricting myself to the quotation just given. Although in the pages that follow, Chomsky amplifies the views about competence set forth in this paragraph, he does not amplify them in a way that satisfies the Humean standards stated at the beginning of this lecture. Because a number of psychologists who have influence in education have been much impressed by Chomsky's notion of competence, it will be useful to examine what he has said and the concept itself in somewhat more detail. It is the most elegant of the fantasies I have evoked and therefore the appropriate one for final consideration.

Let me begin with a key sentence of Chomsky's remarks that is characteristic of conceptual fantasies. After describing the nature of behavioral psychology, he says, "but a generative grammar *cannot* be characterized in these terms." He goes on to say that behavioral psychology has accepted methodological restrictions that do not permit the study of systems of the appropriate complexity. The fantasy consists in this negative claim that a generative grammar *cannot* be characterized within the framework of behavioral psychology. I have on another occasion (Suppes, 1968) criticized a similar claim by Bever, Fodor, and Garrett (1968), who attempted to offer what they consider a formal proof of the limitations of associationism as a basis for language learning. In criticizing their work I characterized it as an example of negative dogma as contrasted to negative proof.

The fantasy claim is especially appropriate in matters of this kind, because

[3] From *Language and Mind,* by Noam Chomsky (New York: Harcourt Brace Jovanovich, 1972). Reprinted by permission of the author and the publisher.

of the long and classical tradition in mathematics of converting negative dogma into negative arguments and establishing thereby a subject of much intellectual richness. To transpose the situation slightly, I can imagine without difficulty the sardonic grin with which a mathematician at Alexandria in, let us say, 100 B.C. would have greeted the unsupported claim that it is obvious that the trisection of an angle cannot be characterized in terms of operations performable by a straightedge and compass alone. A two-word response would have been sufficient: Prove it. The austerity and precision of negative mathematical arguments are too restraining and perhaps puritanical in their methods for Chomsky and his ardent followers.

To give a negative proof, we must first have a much clearer idea of what is meant by the theory of competence than the characterizations given by Chomsky or his cohorts. If we are talking about language, for example, it is strange and wonderful to find only grammar and not semantics mentioned in the discussion of competence. By example we are told that generative grammars provide a model for theories of competence, but what is the model of semantic competence? On the one hand, we are urged not to consider arbitrary grammars and permit thereby the generation of any recursively enumerable set; rather, we should pick grammars with appropriate restrictions. On the other hand, we are told that it is no part of a theory of competence to build in a model of human memory and perception and to deal with it in terms of competence ideas. Reflection on the passages cited and similar writings by linguists in the Chomsky tradition does not give one confidence that a serious intellectual body of ideas is being developed under the heading of the theory of competence.

As my final remark on this, let us even assume that there is such a body of serious ideas to be developed. While there are certain mathematical areas in which one can conceive of formulating what would seem to be a theory of competence, one is struck by how irrelevant it is to any educational or psychological problems.

The mathematical example I want to deal with is that of mathematical proofs. In principle, it is quite straightforward to give a simple-minded theory of competence for mathematical proofs; namely, we know that we can formulate within first-order logic almost all current mathematical ideas, and we can then enumerate the theorems of the subject by enumerating the proofs. The enumeration of the proofs will constitute a kind of theory of competence. Any proof that exists will eventually turn up in the list after only a finite number of predecessors. We have thereby a simple algorithm for the production of any proof, and we can show that abstractly, simply as an algorithm, we can do no better than this.

No one thinks that this formal theory of competence has anything serious to do with the psychology of students' discovering elementary mathematical proofs in elementary mathematical courses or in mathematicians at work in unknown territory discovering new and complex proofs. On the one hand, we give a clear and simple theory of competence, one that we can state much more about in a sharp mathematical fashion than we can in the case of the relation of generative grammars to language; yet, on the other hand, we can all recognize at once the essential irrelevance of this theory of competence to the psychological problems of understanding how someone finds a proof or to the educational problem of providing instruction to students in giving proofs.

It seems to me that there is some reason to conjecture that the relation of this theory of competence for proofs that I have given may bear as close a relation to the proper performance theory of proofs as does current work on generative grammars, especially with a complex transformational component, to correct performance models of language usage. In any case, we certainly need something much more definite and intellectually precise than Chomsky's historical ruminations on the decline and fall of rationalism and its new resurrection under a linguistic flag.

With some regret, I terminate my remarks on fantasies about competence at this point and return to my general theme.


## RESEARCH AND THE BELIEF STRUCTURES OF EDUCATION

I could easily have seized upon a host of lesser targets to provide further case material. Because education is of such universal concern in our society, everyone feels free and often competent to speak about it in general terms. The body of literature full of unsubstantiated general ideas and principles is now overwhelming. Its authors run from the new romantics like Friedenberg and Holt to a bevy of journalists turned sometime scholars. Characteristic of this literature is the lack of intellectual discipline, either in terms of rigorous analysis of general principles or in the presentation of detailed factual evidence to support the principles stated. Unfortunately, this kind of literature represents nothing new in education. The history of educational change is awash with firm prejudices and soggy arguments. I am not, however, an advocate of pessimism or skepticism. I think that it is possible to improve education, and that research can make an increasingly important contribution to this improvement. Let me try to sketch some of the ways I think this can happen.

First of all, it is important to recognize that the belief structure of education, the basis on which decisions about policy and practice are taken, represents an accretion of many years of experience and fantasy. Many of the beliefs are interwoven with other strongly held beliefs about how individual, family, and societal life should be organized. If nothing else, the data of the Coleman report have shown us how difficult it is to isolate any particular effects of education from the broad spectrum of family and cultural influences. A central problem of research is to attack that belief structure where it is unsupported by data or systematic theory. Those of us who do research or defend its relevance are often faced with the task of pointing to instances in which research has had a serious impact on the belief structure of education and, thereby, on actual educational practice.

In my judgment, a number of good examples can be given, almost all of course from the twentieth-century history of educational research, because so little of a systematic nature at all existed before 1900. I do not want, however, to enter into the enumeration of this list, but rather to examine in somewhat more detail the problem of why research does not have more impact on education than it does. Let us take as an example the teaching of reading.

It has been estimated that about 30,000 articles and books have been written about reading since 1920. In this plethora of material certainly a large number of studies report detailed data in a scientifically sophisticated fashion and back up conceptual claims by serious arguments. Why then, it might be asked, is there still so much confusion about methods of teaching reading? Why is there so much disagreement about how reading should be taught? Why do so many articles and books about reading of clearly poor quality still appear?

The answer it seems to me is twofold. On the one hand, the problem of learning to read is a problem that is near at hand for all parents in our society; it is an experience that all of us who are literate have been through. It is a pervasive problem of educational and more generally social-science methodology and research that it is difficult to separate casual unsupported views of the layman from the clearly stated technical and scientific views of the expert. Part of this, I am saying, is due to the closeness of the subject matter to the layman's own experience. The man in the street does not expect to be able to give a serious opinion about how one should build a better television set or a nuclear fuel plant that will reduce pollution. He recognizes, of course, that both of these things are worth having, but he seldom has opinions about how they can be accomplished. In contrast, ask the mother in the street who has a first grader about reading and you are likely to hear some definite views on the teaching of reading.

The nearness of the subject matter is one aspect of the problem, but the other aspect, I think, is a problem about the research itself. Even a casual scientific inspection of the process the child goes through in learning to read quickly demonstrates its complexity. The perceptual, cognitive, linguistic, and motivational aspects of the process are each enormously complicated, and a detailed conception of how the visual perception of what the child sees is related to the spoken language he already knows is far from available. If we compare this situation to the task of improving television sets, the picture is rather dismal. The fundamental physics of the processes involved in projecting a televised image on a screen are well understood; many of the fundamental concepts go back to classical electromagnetic theory of the nineteenth century.

We have in psychology no comparable fundamental theory of perception, nor do we have a comparable theory of spoken language comprehension or production. At the present time, in solving problems of learning to read, we are more in the position of bridge builders before the theory of statics was developed than we are in the position of designers of television sets. It is my own view that no matter how beautiful the Latin squares of experimental design, purely empirical studies of different methods of teaching reading will not solve the problem of giving us the best possible methods, any more than a similarly purely empirical approach would ever have led us from the non-electronic world of 1870 to the electronic marvels of the 1970s. By this remark I do not mean to denigrate the many good empirical studies that have been made of reading, but I do wish to put in perspective the severe limitations we face in practice in the absence of a deeper running theory of the processes involved.

To build such a theory is a good example of a major relevant problem for research in education. Like most research problems in education, the solution cannot depend upon the work solely of persons working in education, but rather it must draw upon scientific results from many disciplines, in this case ranging from neurophysiology through psychology to linguistics. What I consider important as a first step is the recognition that we do not have a fundamental theory of the reading process, and in all likelihood we shall not for some time to come. Let me be a little more explicit about what I mean by a *fundamental theory of the reading process*. I have in mind a theory that not only can predict errors or difficulties of students, but a theory that postulates structures rich enough to process information in the same sequence of steps a student does. Put another way, the models of the fundamental theory should be complete models of the student, and the sense of completeness I use can be given precision by using concepts from logic and computer science.

What I have said about reading applies to most other skills and subjects taught in our schools and colleges. I emphasize that I mean to sound a note of honesty, not of pessimism. Above all, I think the time has come to call for a much deeper theoretical orientation of research in education in order thereby to increase its relevance. In many areas, ranging from the teaching of reading to the teaching of civics, the greatest limitation on research is not the absence of hard-data studies, but the absence of serious and sophisticated theory. Of course, we cannot hope to build a mathematical and quantitative theory of educational processes overnight. We can begin, however, to recognize clearly the absence of fundamental theory and to insist on the kind of intellectual discipline in the training of our graduate students that will give them the tools not merely to make well-designed experimental studies, but to construct well-put-together theories that have definite and precise assumptions and deductive consequences that bear on behavior and the way students learn.

In important ways a good beginning already exists. I would mention especially the statistical theory of tests, the theory of measurement, some parts of learning theory, and recent economic work on productivity in education. Most pressingly needed are mathematical and quantitative theories applicable to major areas of curriculum. In certain areas I see the possibility of rapid advance once a cadre of sufficiently sophisticated research workers is available. In elementary-mathematics education the well-defined structure of the subject and the long tradition of good empirical studies, as well as the modern theory of algorithms and abstract machine processes, make available a welter of concepts and intellectual tools for the development of a fundamental theory of mathematics learning and performance at the elementary school level. To some extent, the same is true of second-language learning, although there is not the same tradition of 50 years of careful studies as there is in the case of elementary mathematics. Other areas that involve complex perceptual or cognitive processes are less amenable to any direct theoretical attack as yet, and it will undoubtedly be some time before even reasonable looking theories, let alone correct ones, are formulated.


## A RESEARCH EXAMPLE FROM ELEMENTARY MATHEMATICS

I recognize, as does everyone else, that it is much easier to criticize than to produce definite constructive results in any area of scientific investigation. My original intention was to give as a final example of a fantasy some excerpts from my own past writings, because the sins of fantasy I have charged others with I have also committed myself in the past. Even worse, I forecast that I shall commit them again in the future.

After further reflection, I decided it would be more useful and, in a deeper sense, expose better my own biases and weaknesses, to sketch in a constructive fashion how a precise theoretical attack on problems of educational relevance can be made. The curriculum I consider is standard and elementary, namely, the algorithms children are taught for performing the basic arithmetical operations of addition, subtraction, multiplication, and division. Also, I first consider performance data and only later say something about learning. Since the detailed theory of these matters is relatively technical, I have put the formal developments in the Appendix (p. 29).

The psychological study of arithmetic skills, like most other parts of psychology, has a relatively recent history—only a few systematic studies were made before 1890. The real impetus was provided by E. L. Thorndike's analysis of the learning of arithmetic in his *Educational Psychology* (1913,

1914) and later in his *The Psychology of Arithmetic* (1922). In an attempt to account for the acquisition of arithmetic skills in terms of his three psychological laws—the law of readiness, the law of exercise, and the law of effect—he tried to justify and analyze the reason for the traditional importance attached to drill and practice in arithmetic; for him the psychological purpose of drill is to strengthen the bonds between stimuli and appropriate responses. He moved on from such fundamental questions to the more practical ones of amount and distribution of practice. He emphasized the advantages of distributed practice and criticized the actual distribution of practice in textbooks of his time. Some effects of his work on the revisions of textbooks in the 1920s and later are documented in Cronbach and Suppes (1969, pp. 103–110).

In the Twenties and Thirties there were a large number of good empirical studies of arithmetic skills, many of which were concerned with detailed questions that had to be answered in any complete psychological theory of arithmetic. For example, Buckingham (1925) studied student preferences and aptitudes for adding up or down in column addition problems. An extensive review of this literature may be found in Suppes, Jerman, and Brian (1968).

Empirical studies like those of Buckingham were not designed to develop an overall theory of arithmetic skills; nor, it is probably fair to say, was Thorndike completely sensitive to the gap that existed between his theoretical ideas and the actual algorithms students were taught to solve problems. There are many stages to work through in developing an adequate theory and, so far as I can see, there is no one point at which one can say the theory is now complete in all respects. If, for example, the theory is adequate at some conceptual level of information processing, then it is possible to move on to additional perceptual questions. Moreover, once a perceptual theory of a certain level of abstraction is successfully developed, it is possible to go on to still more detailed perceptual questions, such as requiring the theory to include eye movements of students as well as their numerical responses. It is for me an important methodological precept that at no foreseeable point shall we reach a fixed and firm bottom beyond which we cannot probe for further details and a more refined theory.

I would like to briefly sketch the history of some work of mine and my younger collaborators over the past six or seven years. Rather than attempt a general coverage, I have decided to select a singular example—the simple one of column addition—to illustrate how we have tried continually to deepen the theory, and then to discuss what I see as yet undone, but practically possible in the near future.

The data referred to are all taken from our work in computer-assisted instruction, but I shall not enter into any of the details. The kinds of models discussed can be applied to students using pencil and paper.

The first question we tried to answer was, how can one predict the relative difficulty of different exercises of column addition? If, for example, we consider problems up to the size of three columns and three rows, we are confronted with approximately one billion problems. A meaningful theory must drastically reduce this large number of exercises to a small number of classes in which all members of a class are essentially the same in difficulty.

Our first approach (Suppes, Hyman, and Jerman, 1967) was to identify a small number of structural features that would permit us to apply linear regression models to predict either probability of correct response or expected latency of response. Additional applications of such regression models may be found in Suppes, Jerman, and Brian (1968) and Suppes and Morningstar (1972). The application of such regression models is exemplified in equation (3) of the Appendix. As can be seen from the information given there, the fit of the regression model to mean student-response data on column addition exercises is not bad. Conceptually, however, there are obvious *lacunae*. The regression model that predicts response probabilities does not really postulate a specific process by which students apply an algorithm to solve an exercise.

The next level of theory developed is aimed precisely at offering such process models, models that satisfy the information-processing requirements laid down for reading models in the earlier discussion. Without doubt, providing an adequate information-processing model for column addition is a much simpler affair than providing one for reading, and I have no illusions about the difference in complexity. The natural theoretical tools for providing process models of algorithmic tasks are automata, and for most of elementary arithmetic simple finite automata are satisfactory. There is, however, one weakness in finite automata as ordinarily defined, namely, they have no place for a probabilistic theory of error, so the natural step is to move from finite deterministic automata to probabilistic automata.

An automaton becomes probabilistic by making the transition function from state to state probabilistic in character. Thus, from a given input and a given internal state there is a probability of going to any one of several different states. In general one wants to make the output function probabilistic also. This means that given an internal state and an input there is a probability distribution over the next output. (These ideas are made formally definite in Definitions 1 and 2 of the Appendix.) By drastically reducing the source of error to a small number of parameters, we can develop and apply manageable probabilistic automata to student-response data. A detailed example including maximum-likelihood estimates of the three parameters of the automaton are given in the Appendix.

Such a probabilistic automaton model takes a definite step beyond a regression model in providing in an abstract sense an adequate information-processing model. From a psychological standpoint, on the other hand, the automaton models described in the Appendix are unsatisfactory in that they lack any perceptual components, and therefore they do not deal directly with how the student actually processes the format of written symbols in front of him.

Our current work is very much directed at this point. In principle, it would be possible to continue the development of automaton models with an abstract concept of state to represent the student's perceptual processing. A weakness of this extension of the automaton models is that when the states are left in a general abstract formulation it is natural to end up designing a different automaton for each of the different tasks in elementary mathematics, and a plethora of models results. Closer examination of the algorithmic tasks of arithmetic facing the student in solving exercises indicates that the various tasks have much in common. This commonality suggests a somewhat different approach, an approach via register machines with perceptual instructions.

Register machines were first introduced by Shepherdson and Sturgis (1963) to give a natural representation of computable functions in terms that are closer to the idea of a computer accepting instructions than to a Turing machine. In the case of the representation of computable functions, a rather simple set of arithmetic instructions is sufficient. In particular, an unlimited register machine has a denumerable sequence of registers, but any given program only uses a finite number of these registers and the machine accepts six basic instructions: add one to a register, subtract one, clear a register, copy from one register to another, and two jump instructions, one conditional and one not. (This set of six instructions is not minimal, but it is convenient.) Obviously, for the perceptual processing that a student does we want a different register machine and a radically different set of instructions. In addition, it is natural to postulate only a finite fixed number of registers that the student can use.

The basic idea of this approach is to drastically simplify the perceptual situation by conceiving each exercise as being presented on a grid. The student is represented by a model that has instructions for attending to a given square on the grid; for example, in the standard algorithms of addition, subtraction, and multiplication we begin in the upper right-hand corner and then have instructions to move downward through each column and from right to left across columns. Additional instructions for storing the results of an operation, for outputting the last digit of a stored numeral, etc., are needed. Some further details are given in the Appendix, but the discussion is not as complete as that for automaton models.

The basic idea of register machines is that the different algorithms are represented by subroutines. One subroutine may be called in another, as complex routines are built up. The procedure is familiar to most of us, even if the language I am using is not. For example, in performing column multiplication we use the algorithm of addition, which in this case means calling the subroutine for addition; in long division we call the subroutines for subtraction and multiplication, as well as for addition. Each basic subroutine is represented by a program in terms of the primitive instructions. The problem from a psychological standpoint is to find instructions that provide not only a realistic description of *what* the student does, a description that can be fitted to data in the same way that the automaton models have been applied to data, but also a fuller account of how the student processes the exercise.

At the first stage of analyzing register-machine models we can get results similar to those for the automaton models by postulating error parameters for execution of main subroutines of the routine for a given algorithm. More is said about this in the Appendix. However, the real purpose of the register machines, in addition to providing some explicit analysis of perceptual processing, is to provide a natural method for analyzing learning.

The approach we have adopted is this. At each given stage, the student has command of a certain set of subroutines or procedures. To master more complex exercises and concepts the student must expand these subroutines or imbed them in more complex ones. A plausible approach is that the student builds up these more complex routines by verbal instruction received from the teacher and by interpretation, especially perceptual interpretation, of examples. When the verbal instruction by the teacher or, say, a computer-assisted instruction program, is explicit, and the link to the necessary internal instructions is close, a surprisingly simple theory of learning within a classical framework can be given. For example, the kind of determinate reinforcement for obtaining finite automata from stimulus-response models, as developed theoretically in Suppes (1969), can without much modification provide the theory for the buildup of the appropriate subroutines.

I emphasize, however, that we are only beginning the detailed analysis of learning in this complex setting, and I am describing the conceptual situation. I shall have to wait until later to report on the actual empirical accuracy of the learning models we have developed. The empirical results obtained with automaton models of performance have been good enough to encourage us to push on as rapidly as possible to the deeper problems of learning.

In this section I have tried to sketch an example of how one can pursue a systematic theory of relevance to education. It should be apparent to everyone that the example I have chosen is exceedingly limited, and from many people's standpoint it is an almost trivial part of the curriculum. On the other hand, it should be equally apparent that the psychological theory of learning and performance in a subject matter as simple even as elementary arithmetic is not in itself simple. In fact, a detailed learning theory of elementary arithmetic is far more complex than the usual kind of theory psychologists consider. One of the problems we have to face in education is the too great willingness of psychologists and others to generalize from quite simple tasks to complex ones.

What I hope to have brought out in the present discussion, which is developed technically in the Appendix, is that the problems of subject-matter learning require conceptual developments in their own right that do not fall naturally out of general ideas of current psychological theories. Yet, with proper use of the variety of conceptual tools now available, it does seem possible to provide an increasingly adequate theory of learning for at least the basic skills, for instance, the basic skills of mathematics and language, that constitute a fair portion of school curriculum everywhere in the world.

## CONCLUSION

I would like to conclude with a final remark about theory construction relevant to education. The times have probably never been so propitious for luring some of the ablest young minds into the problems of educational research. There exists already a body of methods and results of which we can be proud; but it is also clear, especially when we turn to the construction of systematic theories of learning or instruction, that we have as yet scarcely scratched the surface. While we are scratching that surface those of us in educational research must impose exacting standards not only on ourselves, but also on our neighbors, be they linguists or psychologists. We must demand of them, as well as of ourselves, the best possible effort in theory construction. We must above all reject the attitude that has in the past sometimes been prevalent that second-rate theories and second-rate efforts in the development of theory will suffice for education, and that we are lucky to get small crumbs from the occasional psychologist or linguist or economist who happens to become interested in education. We do not need ill-worked-out theories from other disciplines. We do not need fantasies of abstractions and platitudes unsupported by serious and rigorous development. What we need for relevance in education are theories of intellectual power and rigor, and we should not rest until we get them.

## APPENDIX [4]

In this appendix I give some (but by no means all) of the technical details of our research in the psychology of arithmetic. The first three sections deal with performance models and the last section deals with a learning model. Each section attempts to dig a step deeper than its predecessor into the skills of arithmetic. For simplicity I have restricted the analysis in this appendix to the simple case of column addition, but the methods either already have been or in principle can be extended to essentially the entire domain of elementary school mathematics (in addition to the references in the main text, see Groen

[4] The research reported in the Appendix has been supported by the National Science Foundation Grant NSFGJ–443X and U. S. Office of Education Grant OEG–970–0024(057).

and Parkman, 1972; Suppes and Groen, 1967). On the other hand, a good many additional developments will be needed to extend this work even to routine parts of the undergraduate college mathematics curriculum. (Some very empirical first steps at this college level are to be found in Goldberg and Suppes, 1972; Kane, 1972; Moloney, 1972.)

### Linear Regression Models

As mentioned in the main text I begin with regression models that use as independent variables structural features of individual arithmetic exercises. I denote the $j$th structural feature of exercise $i$ in a given set of exercises by $f_{ij}$. The parameters estimated from the data are the values attached to each structural feature. (In previous publications we have referred to these structural features as factors, but this can lead to confusion with the concept of factor as used in factor analysis.) I denote the coefficient assigned to the $j$th structural feature by $a_j$, and I emphasize that the structural features themselves, as opposed to their coefficients, are objectively identifiable by the experimenter in terms of the exercises themselves, independent of the response data.

Let $p_i$ be the observed proportion of correct responses on exercise $i$ for a given group of students. The natural linear regression in terms of the structural features $f_{ij}$ and the coefficients $a_j$ is simply

$$p_i = \sum_j a_j f_{ij} + a_0.$$

Unfortunately, when the regression is put in this form, there is no guarantee that probability will be preserved as the structural features are combined to predict the observed proportion of correct responses. To guarantee conservation of probability, it is natural to make the following transformation and to define a new variable $z_i$.

$$(1) \qquad z_i = \log \frac{1 - p_i}{p_i},$$

and then to use as the regression model

$$(2) \qquad z_i = \sum_j a_j f_{ij} + a_0.$$

The numerator of equation (1) contains $1 - p_i$ rather than $p_i$, so that the variable $z_i$ increases monotonically rather than decreases monotonically with the magnitude of the structural features $f_{ij}$.

In Chapter 3 of Suppes and Morningstar (1972), the following structural features were defined for column-addition exercises.

The feature SUMR is the number of columns in the largest addend. For three-row exercises SUMR is defined as 1.5 times the number of columns, plus .5 if a column is 20 or more. For example,

$$\text{SUMR}\ (\overset{a}{\underset{c}{+b}}) = 1$$

$$\text{SUMR}\ (\begin{matrix} a \\ b \\ \underline{+\ c} \\ de \end{matrix}) = \left\{ \begin{matrix} 1.5 \text{ if } de < 20 \\ 2 \ \ \text{ if } de \geqq 20 \end{matrix} \right.$$

$$\text{SUMR}\ (\underline{ab} + c = \underline{de}) = 2.$$

This structural feature reflects the number of columns of addition, with greater weight being given to columns in three-row exercises than in two-row exercises.

The second structural feature is CAR, which represents the number of times the sum of a column, including any numbers carried to it, exceeds nine. For example,

$$\text{CAR}\ (\overset{a}{\underset{c}{+b}}) = 0$$

$$\text{CAR}\ (a + b = \underline{cd}) = 1$$

$$\text{CAR}\ (\overset{ab}{\underset{ef}{+cd}}) = \left\{ \begin{matrix} 0 \text{ if } b + d \leqq 9 \\ 1 \text{ if } b + d > 9 \end{matrix} \right.$$

$$\text{CAR}\ (\begin{matrix} ab \\ cd \\ \underline{+\ ef} \\ ghi \end{matrix}) = \left\{ \begin{matrix} 1 \text{ if } b + d + f \leqq 9,\ a + c + e > 9 \\ 2 \text{ if } b + d + f > 9,\ a + c + e \geqq 9. \end{matrix} \right.$$

The third structural feature VF reflects the vertical format of the exercise. The vertical exercises with one-digit responses were given the value 0. Multi-column exercises with multidigit exercises and one-column addition exercises with a response of 11 were given the value 1. One-column addition exercises with a multidigit response other than 11 were given the value 3. For example,

$$\text{VF}\ (\overset{ab}{\underset{e}{-cd}}) = 0$$

$$\text{VF}\ (\overset{abc}{\underset{ghi}{+def}}) = 1$$

$$\text{VF}\ (\overset{a}{\underset{cd}{+\ b}}) = 3.$$

This structural feature is meant to reflect the likelihood of the mistake of reversing the digits of the correct response, especially in a one-column addition exercise. In the computer-assisted instruction environment where students were responding at teletype terminals, responses to vertical exercises were typed from right to left, while responses to horizontal exercises were typed from left to right. Thus, it was possible for a student to have in mind the correct answer, but to err by typing the digits in the reverse order. It is fair to say that this structural feature is of more importance in working at a computer-based terminal than when using paper and pencil.

Table 1 shows a pretest on column addition given to third graders. The following regression equation was obtained for the mean response data of 63 students taking the test.

(3)        $p_i = .53 \, SUMR_i + .93 \, CAR_i + .31 \, VF_i - 4.06.$

### Table 1

#### PRETEST EXERCISES IN COLUMN ADDITION

| 1)  | 17<br>+ 2 | 8)  | 11<br>22<br>+ 14 | 15) | 5267<br>+ 283 |
|-----|-----------|-----|------------------|-----|---------------|
| 2)  | 6<br>6<br>+ 5 | 9)  | 27<br>+ 4 | 16) | 46<br>75<br>+ 23 |
| 3)  | 14<br>+ 15 | 10) | 8<br>+ 32 | 17) | 3986<br>+ 4735 |
| 4)  | 6<br>+ 13 | 11) | 639<br>+ 212 | 18) | 27<br>46<br>+ 88 |
| 5)  | 363<br>+ 214 | 12) | 66<br>+ 14 | 19) | 7657<br>+ 1875 |
| 6)  | 416<br>+ 212 | 13) | 378<br>+ 125 | 20) | 69<br>36<br>+ 48 |
| 7)  | 12<br>31<br>+ 10 | 14) | 557<br>+ 256 |     |  |

The multiple R was .74 and $R^2$ was .54, which reflects a reasonable fit to the data. I shall not enter into further details of the regression model, but shall move on to the next level of analysis of these same response data. As should be obvious, I am not attempting anything like a systematic presentation of data, but only enough to give a sense of how some of the models do fit.

### Three-State Automaton Model

The central weakness of the regression models is that they are not process models. They do not provide even a schematic analysis of the algorithmic steps the student uses to find an answer. Automaton models are process models and therefore their use represents a natural extension of the regression analysis. For the exercises in column addition we may restrict ourselves to finite automata, but as ordinarily defined they have no place for errors. However, this is easily introduced by moving from deterministic state transitions to probabilistic ones.

I begin with the definition of a finite deterministic automaton, and then generalize. These developments follow Suppes (1969).

*Definition 1.   A structure* $\mathfrak{U} = <A,V_I,V_0,M,Q,s_0>$ *is a finite (deterministic) automaton with output if and only if*

(i)   *A is a finite, nonempty set,*

(ii)   $V_I$ *and* $V_0$ *are finite nonempty sets (the input and output vocabularies, respectively),*

(iii)   *M is a function from the Cartesian product* $A \times V_I$ *to A (M defines the transition table),*

(iv)   *Q is a function from the Cartesian product* $A \times V_I$ *to* $V_0$ *(Q is the output function),*

(v)   $s_0$ *is in A* ($s_0$ *is the initial state).*

As an example of a finite automaton with output, that is, a finite automaton in the sense of this definition, we may characterize an automaton that will perform two-row column addition.

$$A = \{0,1\},$$
$$V_I = \{(m,n) : 0 \leq m,\ n \leq 9\},$$
$$V_0 = \{0,1,\ldots,9\},$$
$$M(k,(m,n)) = \begin{cases} 0 \text{ if } m + n + k \leq 9, \\ 1 \text{ if } m + n + k > 9, \end{cases} \text{ for } k = 0,1,$$
$$Q(k,(m,n)) = (k + m + n) \bmod 10,$$
$$s_0 = 0.$$

Thus the automaton operates by adding first the ones' column, storing as internal state 0 if there is no carry, 1 if there is a carry, outputting the sum of the ones' column modulus 10, and then moving on to the input of the two tens' column digits, etc. The initial internal state $s_0$ is 0, because at the beginning of the exercise there is no "carry."

Definition 2.    A structure $\mathfrak{A} = <A,V_I,V_0,p,q,s_0>$ is a (finite) probabilistic automaton if and only if
(i)    $A$ is a finite, nonempty set,
(ii)    $V_I$ and $V_0$ are finite, nonempty sets,
(iii)    $p$ is a function on $A \times V \times A$ to the interval $[0,1]$ such that for each $s$ in $A$ and $\sigma$ in $V$, $p_{s,o}$ is a probability density over $A$, i.e.,
(a)    for each $s'$ in $A$, $p_{s,o}(s') \geqq 0$,
(b)    $\sum\limits_{s' \epsilon A} p_{s,o}(s') = 1$,
(iv)    $q$ is a function on $A \times V_I \times V_0$ to $[0,1]$ such that for each $s$ in $A$ and $\sigma$ in $V$, $q_{s,o}$ is a probability density over $V_0$,
(v)    $s_0$ is in $A$.

In the probabilistic generalization of the automaton for column addition, the number of possible parameters that can be introduced is uninterestingly large. Each transition $M(k, (m,n))$ may be replaced by a probabilistic transition $1 - \epsilon_{k,m,n}$ and $\epsilon_{k,m,n}$ and each output $Q(k(m,n))$, by 10 probabilities for a total of 2200 parameters.

A three-parameter automaton model structurally rather close to the regression model is easily defined. First, two parameters, $\epsilon$ and $\eta$, are introduced according to whether there is a "carry" to the next column.

$$P(M(k,(m,n)) = 0 \mid k + m + n \leqq 9) = 1 - \epsilon$$

and

$$P(M(k,(m,n)) = 1 \mid k + m + n > 9) = 1 - \eta.$$

In other words, if there is no "carry," the probability of a correct transition is $1 - \epsilon$ and if there is a "carry" the probability of such a transition is $1 - \eta$. The third parameter, $\gamma$, is simply the probability of an output error. Conversely, the probability of a correct output is:

$$P(Q(k,(m,n)) = (k + m + n) \bmod 10) = 1 - \gamma.$$

Consider now exercise $i$ with $C_i$ carrys and $D_i$ digits. If we ignore the probability of two errors leading to a correct response (e.g., a transition error followed by an output error), then the probability of a correct answer is just

(4)    $P$(Correct Answer to Exercise $i$)
$$= (1 - \gamma)^{D_i}(1 - \eta)^{C_i}(1 - \epsilon)^{D_i-C_i-1}.$$

As already indicated, it is important to realize that this equation is an approximation of the "true" probability. However, to compute the exact probability it is necessary to make a definite assumption about how the probability $\gamma$ of an output error is distributed among the nine possible wrong responses. A simple and intuitively appealing one-parameter model is the one that arranges the 10 digits on a circle in natural order with 9 next to 0, and then makes the probability of an error $j$ steps to the right or left of the correct response $\delta^j$. For example, if 5 is the correct digit, then the probability of responding 4 is $\delta$, of 3 is $\delta^2$, of 2 is $\delta^3$, of 1 is $\delta^4$, of 0 is $\delta^5$, of 6 is $\delta$, of 7 is $\delta^2$, etc. Thus in terms of the original model

$$\gamma = 2(\delta + \delta^2 + \delta^3 + \delta^4) + \delta^5.$$

Consider now the exercise

$$\begin{array}{r} 47 \\ + 15 \\ \hline \end{array}$$

Then, where $d_i$ = the $i^{\text{th}}$ digit response,

$$P(d_1 = 2) = (1 - \gamma),$$
$$P(d_2 = 6) = (1 - \gamma)(1 - \eta) + \eta\delta.$$

Here the additional term is $\eta\delta$, because if the state entered is 0 rather than 1 when the pair $(7,5)$ is input, the only way of obtaining a correct answer is for 6 to be given as the sum of $0 + 4 + 1$, which has a probability $\delta$. Thus the probability of a correct response to this exercise is $(1 - \gamma)[(1 - \gamma)(1 - \eta) + \eta\delta]$. Hereafter we shall ignore the $\eta\delta$ (or $\epsilon\delta$) terms.

Returning to (4) we may get a direct comparison with the linear regression model defined by (3), if we take the logarithm of both sides to obtain:

(5)   $\log p_i = D_i \log(1 - \gamma) + C_i \log(1 - \eta) + (D_i - C_i - 1)\log(1 - \epsilon),$

and estimate $\log 1 - \gamma$, $\log 1 - \eta$, and $\log 1 - \epsilon$ by regression with the additive constant set equal to zero. We also may use some other approach to estimation such as minimum $\chi^2$ or maximum likelihood. An analytic solution of the standard maximum-likelihood equations is difficult, but the maximum of the likelihood function can be found numerically.

The automaton model naturally suggests a more detailed analysis of the data. Unlike the regression model, the automaton provides an immediate analysis of the digit-by-digit responses. Ignoring the $\epsilon\delta$-type terms, we can in fact find the general maximum-likelihood estimates of $\gamma$, $\epsilon$, and $\eta$ when the response data are given in this more explicit form.

Let there be $n$ digit responses in a block of exercises. For $1 \leq i \leq n$ let $x_i$ be the random variable that assumes the value 1 if the $i^{\text{th}}$ response is correct and 0 otherwise. It is then easy to see that

$$P(x_i = 1) = \begin{cases} (1 - \gamma) & \text{if } i \text{ is a ones'-column digit,} \\ (1 - \gamma)(1 - \epsilon) & \text{if it is not a ones' column and there} \\ & \text{is no carry to the } i^{\text{th}} \text{ digit,} \\ (1 - \gamma)(1 - \eta) & \text{if there is a carry to the } i^{\text{th}} \text{ digit,} \end{cases}$$

granted that $\epsilon\delta$-type terms are ignored. Similarly for the same three alternatives

$$P(x_i = 0) = \begin{cases} \gamma \\ 1 - (1 - \gamma)(1 - \epsilon) \\ 1 - (1 - \gamma)(1 - \eta). \end{cases}$$

So for a string of actual digit responses $x_1, \ldots, x_n$ we can write the likelihood function as:

(6)     $L(x_1, \ldots, x_n) =$
$$(1 - \gamma)^a \gamma^b (1 - \epsilon)^c (1 - \eta)^d [1 - (1 - \gamma)(1 - \epsilon)]^e [1 - (1 - \gamma)(1 - \eta)]^f,$$

where $a$ = number of correct responses, $b$ = number of incorrect responses in the ones' column, $c$ = number of correct responses not in the ones' column when the internal state is 0, $d$ = number of correct responses when the internal state is 1, $e$ = number of incorrect responses not in the ones' column when the internal state is 0, and $f$ = number of incorrect responses when the internal state is 1. (In the model, statistical independence of responses is assured by the correction procedure.) It is more convenient to estimate $\gamma'$ $= 1 - \gamma$, $\epsilon' = 1 - \epsilon$, and $\eta' = 1 - \eta$. Making this change, taking the logarithm of both sides of (6) and differentiating with respect to each of the variables, we obtain three equations that determine the maximum-likelihood estimates of $\gamma'$, $\epsilon'$, and $\eta'$:

$$\frac{\partial L}{\partial \gamma'} = \frac{a}{\gamma'} - \frac{b}{1 - \gamma'} - \frac{e\epsilon'}{1 - \gamma'\epsilon'} - \frac{f\eta'}{1 - \gamma'\eta'} = 0,$$

$$\frac{\partial L}{\partial \epsilon'} = \frac{c}{\epsilon'} - \frac{e\gamma'}{1 - \gamma'\epsilon'} = 0,$$

$$\frac{\partial L}{\partial \eta'} = \frac{d}{\eta'} - \frac{f\gamma'}{1 - \gamma'\eta'} = 0.$$

Solving these equations, we obtain as estimates:

$$\gamma' = \frac{a - c - d}{a + b - c - d},$$

$$\epsilon' = \frac{c(a + b - c - d)}{(c + e)(a - c - d)},$$

$$\hat{\eta} = \frac{d(a + b - c - d)}{(d + f)(a - c - d)}.$$

Estimates of the parameters for the same third-grade data already described, as well as a graph of the observed and predicted response probabilities for the exercises shown in Table 1, are given in Chapter 4 of Suppes and Morningstar (1972). (This chapter was written in collaboration with Alex Cannara and he is responsible for the data analysis.) The estimates are: $\gamma = .0430$,

$\hat{\epsilon} = .0085$ and $\hat{\eta} = .0576$. The graph of response probabilities is reproduced as Figure 1. A detailed discussion of the fit of the model and further analysis of some of the discrepancies are to be found in the chapter mentioned. Here I have tried only to give a sense of how this kind of model can be brought into direct confrontation with data.

### Register Machines with Perceptual Instructions

To introduce greater generality and to deepen the analysis to include specific ideas about the perceptual processing of a column-addition exercise, I move on to register machines for the reasons described in the third section of the main text, "Research and the Belief Structures of Education." This research is being conducted in collaboration with Lindsay L. Flannery.

For column addition three registers suffice in our scheme of analysis. First there is the stimulus-supported register [SS] that holds an encoded representation of a printed symbol to which the student is perceptually attending. In the present case the alphabet of such symbols consists of the 10 digits and the underline symbol '___'. As a new symbol is attended to, previously stored symbols are lost unless transferred to a non-stimulus-supported register. The second register is the non-stimulus-supported register [NSS]. It provides long-term storage for computational results. The third register is the operations register [OP] that acts as a short-term store, both for encodings of external stimuli and for results of calculations carried out on the contents of other registers. It is also primarily non-stimulus-supported.

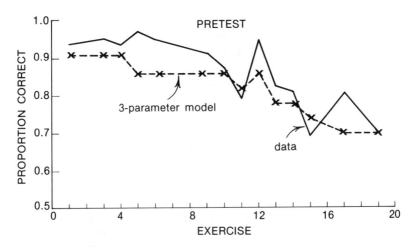

Figure 1.   Predicted and observed probability correct for 3-parameter automaton model.

As already stated in the main text, we drastically simplify the perceptual situation by conceiving each exercise as being presented on a grid with at most one symbol in each square of the grid. For column addition we number the coordinates of the grid from the upper right-hand corner. Thus, in the exercise

$$
\begin{array}{r}
15 \\
24 \\
+\,37 \\
\hline
\end{array}
$$

the coordinates of the digit 5 are (1,1), the coordinates of 4 are (2,1), the coordinates of 7 are (3,1), the coordinates of 1 are (1,2) and so forth, with the first coordinate being the row number and the second being the column number.

The restricted set of instructions we need for column addition are the following ten.

| | |
|---|---|
| Attend (a,b): | Direct attention to grid position (a,b). |
| (±a, ±b): | Shift attention on the grid by (±a, ±b). |
| Readin [SS]: | Read into the stimulus-supported register the physical symbol in the grid position addressed by Attend. |
| Lookup [R1] + [R2]: | Look up table of basic addition facts for adding contents of register [R1] and [R2] and store the result in [R1]. |
| Copy [R1] in [R2]: | Copy the content of register [R1] in register [R2]. |
| Deleteright [R]: | Delete the rightmost symbol of register [R]. |
| Jump L: | Jump to line labeled L. |
| Jump (val) R,L: | Jump to line labeled L if content of register [R] is val. |
| Outright [R]: | Write (output) the rightmost symbol of register [R] at grid position addressed by Attend. |
| End: | Terminate processing of current exercise. |
| Exit: | Terminate subroutine processing and return to next line of main program. |

Of the ten instructions only *Lookup* does not have an elementary character. In our complete analysis it has the status of a subroutine built up from more primitive operations such as those of counting. It is, of course, more than a problem of constructing the table of basic addition facts from counting subroutines; it is also a matter of being able to add a single digit to any number stored in the non-stimulus-supported register [NSS] or [OP], as, for exam-

ple, in adding many rows of digits in a given column. I omit the details of
building up this subroutine.

It should also be obvious that the remaining nine instructions are not a
minimal set; for example, the unconditional jump instruction is easily elimi-
nated. We do think the nine are both elementary and psychologically intui-
tive for the subject matter at hand.

To illustrate in a simple way the use of subroutines, we may consider two
that are useful in writing the program for column addition. The first is the
*vertical scan* subroutine, which is needed for the following purpose. In adding
rows of numbers with an uneven number of digits, we cannot simply stop
when we reach a blank grid square on the left of the topmost row. We must
also scan downward to see if there are digits in that column in any other row.
A second aspect of this same problem is that in our model the student is
perceptually processing only one grid square at a time, so that he must have
a check for finding the bottom row by looking continually for an underline
symbol. Otherwise he could, according to an apparently natural subroutine,
proceed indefinitely far downward encountering only blanks and leaving entirely the immediate perceptual region of the formatted exercise. Here is the
subroutine. In the main program it is preceded by an Attend instruction.

### VERTICAL SCAN SUBROUTINE

```
V-scan (0-9,___)
    Rd          Readin
                Jump (0-9,___) SS, Fin
                Attend (+1,-1)
                Readin
                Jump (___) SS, Fin
                Attend (+0,+1)
                Jump Rd
    Fin         Exit
```

The labels Rd and Fin of two of the lines are shown on the left.

The second subroutine is one that outputs all the digits in a register working from right to left. For example, in column addition, after the leftmost
column has been added, there may still be several digits remaining to print
out to the left of this column in the "answer" row.

```
Output [R]
    Put         Outright [R]
                Deleteright [R]
                Attend (0,+1)
                Jump (Blank) R, Fin
                Jump Put
    Fin         Exit
```

Using these two subroutines the program for vertical addition is relatively straightforward and requires 26 lines. I number the lines for later reference; they are not a part of the program.

### VERTICAL ADDITION

| | | |
|---|---|---|
| 1. | | Attend (1,1) |
| 2. | | Readin |
| 3. | | Copy [SS] in [OP] |
| 4. | | Attend (+1,+0) |
| 5. | | Readin |
| 6. | Opr | Lookup [OP] + [SS] |
| 7. | Rd | Attend (+1,0) |
| 8. | | Readin |
| 9. | | Jump (0–9) SS, Opr |
| 10. | | Jump (Blank) SS, Rd |
| 11. | | Attend (+1,0) |
| 12. | | Outright [OP] |
| 13. | | Deleteright [OP] |
| 14. | | Copy [OP] in [NSS] |
| 15. | | Attend (1,+1) |
| 16. | | V-scan (0–9, __) |
| 17. | | Jump (__) SS, Fin |
| 18. | | Jump (0–9) SS, Car |
| 19. | | Copy [SS] in [OP] |
| 20. | | Jump Rd |
| 21. | Car | Copy [NSS] in [OP] |
| 22. | | Jump Opr |
| 23. | Fin | Jump (Blank) NSS, Out |
| 24. | | Attend (+1,0) |
| 25. | | Output [NSS] |
| 26. | Out | End |

To show how the program works, we may consider a simple one-column addition exercise. I show at the right of each line the content of each register just before the next row is attended to, i.e., after all operations have been performed.

| | [SS] | [OP] | [NSS] |
|---|---|---|---|
| 4 | 4 | 4 | |
| 5 | 5 | 9 | |
| 3 | 3 | 12 | |
| 8 | 8 | 20 | |
| — | — | 20 | |
| 0 | 0 | | 2 |

This kind of analysis can be generalized to prove that the program is correct, i.e., will output the correct answer to any column-addition exercise, but this aspect of matters will not be pursued further here.

By attaching error parameters to various segments of the program, performance models are easily generated. For comparative purposes we may define a performance model essentially identical to the two-state probabilistic automaton already introduced for column addition restricted to two rows. To lines 6–12 we attach the output error parameter $\gamma$, and to lines 13–19 we attach the "carry" error parameter $\eta$ if there is a carry, and the error parameter $\epsilon$ if there is not. Given this characterization of the error parameters the two performance models are behaviorally identical. On the other hand, it is clear that the program for the three-register machine is much more general than the two-state probabilistic automaton, since it is able to solve any vertical addition exercise. It is also obvious that other performance models can easily be defined for vertical addition by introducing error parameters attached to different segments of the program.

### Learning

In an earlier article (Suppes, 1969), I proved that given any connected finite automaton there is a stimulus-response model of learning that is asymptotically isomorphic to the automaton, i.e., as the number of trials approaches infinity, and initially all stimuli may be unconditioned to any of the desired responses. In one clear sense, however, the theorem proved is too weak because of the special character of the reinforcement schedule. What is required is reinforcement of the transitions from each response-stimulus pair to the next response, where the responses, internal or external, constitute the states of the automaton. The response on trial $n$ must become conditioned to the pair consisting of the response of trial $n - 1$ and the stimulus on trial $n$. A complete matching of the reinforcement schedule to such conditioning connections is often not experimentally feasible.

At the other end of the scale, Rottmayer (1970) proved the following theorem. Let C be a classification scheme for dividing a possibly infinite set of stimuli or stimulus patterns into two classes, such that the classification of any pattern can be accomplished by a finite automaton. Then there is a stimulus-response model that can learn the classification scheme C given as reinforcement only the information of whether its classification of successively presented patterns is correct or incorrect. The weakness of this theorem is that the learning is very slow, and machinery for building up a hierarchy of concepts is not directly provided.

The shift from automata to register machines seems promising not only for the development of performance models, but also for the construction of learning models. Learning in this framework consists of building internal programs of increasing complexity. The reinforcement procedures realistically fall between the two extremes described above. Verbal directions and corrections correspond closely, but not exactly, to segments of *an* appropriate program (I emphasize *an* because the internal program constructed is not necessarily unique).

I restrict myself here to an example of this approach. I take as the class of exercises single-column addition, but with an indefinite number of rows. The program is simpler than the general one given above, and it is easy to see the relation between what is said to the student by the teacher or computer to the desired internal program. In Figure 2, I show the verbal instructions on the right with the physical pointing to the relevant part of the displayed exercise

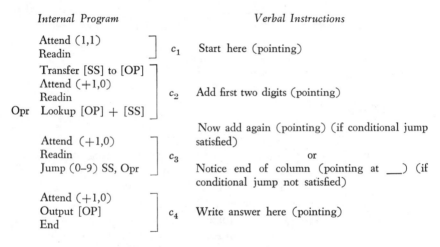

| *Internal Program* | | *Verbal Instructions* |
|---|---|---|
| Attend $(1,1)$ <br> Readin | $c_1$ | Start here (pointing) |
| Transfer [SS] to [OP] <br> Attend $(+1,0)$ <br> Readin <br> Opr   Lookup [OP] + [SS] | $c_2$ | Add first two digits (pointing) |
| Attend $(+1,0)$ <br> Readin <br> Jump (0–9) SS, Opr | $c_3$ | Now add again (pointing) (if conditional jump satisfied) <br> or <br> Notice end of column (pointing at ___) (if conditional jump not satisfied) |
| Attend $(+1,0)$ <br> Output [OP] <br> End | $c_4$ | Write answer here (pointing) |

*Figure 2.   Single-column addition.*

indicated in parentheses. When errors are made, still more detailed instructions, tailored to the particular error, can be given, but I do not consider such error messages here.

In Figure 2, learning parameters $c_1$, $c_2$, $c_3$, and $c_4$ are shown for the four segments of the program. Various learning models can be formulated in terms of these four parameters. The simplest is the one that assumes *independence* of the four parts. If we treat the probability of successive errors combining to yield a correct response as having probability zero, then the mean probability for a correct response on trial $n$ for the independence model is simply:

$$P_n \text{ (Correct Response)} = \prod_{i=1}^{4} (1 - (1 - c_i)^{n-1}).$$

At the other extreme a hierarchical model postulates that the $i^{\text{th}}$ segment of the program cannot be learned until the $i\text{-}1^{\text{st}}$ segment is learned. This hierarchical model leads to the following transition matrix, where state 0 represents all segments as unlearned, state 1 represents the first segment only as learned, etc.

| | 4 | 3 | 2 | 1 | 0 |
|---|---|---|---|---|---|
| 4 | 1 | 0 | 0 | 0 | 0 |
| 3 | $c_4$ | $1-c_4$ | 0 | 0 | 0 |
| 2 | 0 | $c_3$ | $1-c_3$ | 0 | 0 |
| 1 | 0 | 0 | $c_2$ | $1-c_2$ | 0 |
| 0 | 0 | 0 | 0 | $c_1$ | $1-c_1$ |

Detailed comparison of these two models, especially for testing against data, requires considerable further development, but the relevant mathematical and probabilistic techniques are familiar in the literature of mathematical learning theory.

What is missing from a theoretical standpoint is a deeper conceptualization of the relation between verbal instructions and reinforcements on the one hand and the construction of appropriate segments of internal programs on the other. In the example given above, the crucial concept of iteration or recursion embodied in the conditional jump instruction is presumed to be learned from the instruction "Now add again," with *again* mainly carrying the force of the recursion. I hope to have something more to say in the near future about this difficult and important problem.

## REFERENCES

Beilin, H. Developmental stages and developmental processes. In D. R. Green, M. P. Ford, and G. B. Flamer (Eds.), *Measurement and Piaget*. New York: McGraw-Hill, 1971. Pp. 172–197.

Bever, T. G., Fodor, J. A., and Garrett, M. Formal limitation of association. In T. R. Dixon and D. L. Horton (Eds.), *Verbal behavior and general behavior theory*. Englewood Cliffs, N. J.: Prentice-Hall, 1968. Pp. 582–585.

Bloomfield, L., and Barnhart, C. L. *Let's read, a linguistic approach*. Detroit: Wayne State University Press, 1961.

Buckingham, B. R. Adding up or down: A discussion. *Journal of Educational Research*, 1925, *12*, 251–261.

Campbell, D. T., and Stanley, J. C. Experimental and quasi-experimental designs for research. In N. L. Gage (Ed.), *Handbook for research on teaching*. Skokie, Ill.: Rand-McNally, 1963. Pp. 171–246.

Chomsky, N. *Language and mind*. New York: Harcourt Brace Jovanovich, 1972.

Cronbach, L. J., and Suppes, P. (Eds.). *Research for tomorrow's schools*. New York: Macmillan, 1969.

Goldberg, A., and Suppes, P. A computer-assisted instruction program for exercises on finding axioms. *Educational Studies in Mathematics,* 1972 (in press).

Groen, G. J., and Parkman, J. M. A chronometric analysis of simple addition. *Psychological Review,* 1972, 79, 329–343.

Hume, D. *Enquiries concerning human understanding and concerning the principles of morals.* (2nd ed.) Oxford: Clarendon Press, 1902.

Inhelder, B., and Piaget, J. *The early growth of logic in the child.* New York: Harper & Row, 1964. English translation by E. A. Lunzer and D. Papert.

Kane, M. T. Variability in the proof behavior of college students in a CAI course in logic as a function of problem characteristics. Technical Report No. 192, 1972, Stanford University, Institute for Mathematical Studies in the Social Sciences.

Laplace, P. S. *Theorie analytique des probabilities.* Troisième édition revue et augmentée par l'auteur. Paris: Courcier, 1820.

Moloney, J. M. An investigation of college student performance on a logic curriculum in a computer-assisted instruction setting. Technical Report No. 183, 1972, Stanford University, Institute for Mathematical Studies in the Social Sciences.

Piaget, J. Discussion in J. M. Tanner and B. Inhelder (Eds.), *Discussions on child development.* Vol. 4. New York: International Universities Press, 1960.

———. Discussion in D. R. Green, M. P. Ford and G. B. Flamer (Eds.), *Measurement and Piaget.* New York: McGraw-Hill, 1971.

Rottmayer, W. A. A formal theory of perception. Technical Report No. 161, 1970, Stanford University, Institute for Mathematical Studies in the Social Sciences.

Shepherdson, J. C., and Sturgis, H. E. The computability of partial recursive functions. *Journal of the Association of Computing Machinery,* 1963, 10, 217–255.

Skinner, B. F. *The technology of teaching.* New York: Appleton-Century-Crofts, 1968.

Suppes, P. On the behavioral foundations of mathematical concepts. *Monographs of the Society for Research in Child Development,* 1965, 30, 60–96.

———. The desirability of formalization in science. *Journal of Philosophy,* 1968, 65, 651–664.

———. Stimulus-response theory of finite automata. *Journal of Mathematical Psychology,* 1969, 6, 327–355.

———, and Ginsberg, R. A fundamental property of all-or-none models, binomial distribution of responses prior to conditioning, with application to concept formation in children. *Psychological Review,* 1963, 70, 139–161.

———, and Groen, G. J. Some counting models for first grade performance data on simple addition facts. In J. M. Scandura (Ed.), *Research in mathematics education.* Washington, D. C.: National Council of Teachers of Mathematics, 1967. Pp. 35–43.

———, Hyman, L., and Jerman, M. Linear structural models for response and latency performance in arithmetic on computer-controlled terminals. In J. P.

Hill (Ed.), *Minnesota symposia on child psychology*. Minneapolis: University of Minnesota Press, 1967. Pp. 160–200.

———, Jerman, M., and Brian, D. *Computer-assisted instruction: The 1965–66 Stanford arithmetic program*. New York: Academic Press, 1968.

——— and Morningstar, M. *Computer-assisted instruction at Stanford, 1966–68: Data, models, and evaluation of the arithmetic programs*. New York: Academic Press, 1972.

Thorndike, E. L. *Educational psychology*. Vols. 1, 2, 3. New York: Teachers College Press, Columbia University, 1913–1914.

Thorndike, E. L. *The psychology of arithmetic*. New York: Macmillan, 1922.

# II

# ALTERNATIVE CONCEPTIONS OF EDUCATIONAL RESEARCH

# ✺❦ 2 ❧✺

# Freedom Beyond *Beyond Freedom*

## MICHAEL SCRIVEN

### INFORMAL INTRODUCTION

In my view, Skinner's practice has long stood as a powerful paradigm of what psychology should do. Yet, also in my view, his philosophy of psychology has long been a mere monument to the seductive power of ancient fallacies and fantasies. One might reasonably conclude that this shows how irrelevant philosophy of science is to good scientific practice. But I also happen to believe that philosophy of science is the principal intellectual influence on the shape of science, and that improved philosophy of science is almost always productive of improved science. Well, there could be an exception or two. Nevertheless, there is a certain tension between valuing philosophy of science for its contribution to science, valuing Skinner for *his* contribution to science, and believing that his philosophy of science is almost totally wrong. It is the purpose of this paper to reduce this tension.

In the works of the Catholic novelists G. K. Chesterton and Graham Greene, as in the humanist Camus, one often finds that the man of God exhibits a strange fascination with an atheist who seems nevertheless good, and strong, and honest. Does the priest see in him a threat—or a hope? The risk of losing faith, or of gaining a great convert? Whichever it is, he spends more time with the atheist than with any of the more obvious sinners, whose salvation—or even amelioration—would apparently do far more to improve the world. Perhaps that is because those novelists are intellectuals writing

An earlier version of this paper, expanded from this original AERA address, was published in the NSSE *Yearbook on Behavior Modification,* ed. by Carl Thoresen.

49

for intellectuals, and the intellectual is sensitive to the tension between ideology and practice.

At any rate, as a man of no God but with some theology nonetheless, I have found myself closely engaged with Skinner and Skinner's work over the years. Nearly 20 years ago I wrote what may still retain the dubious but quantitative distinction of being the longest study of his work in print.[1] In the years since, I have worked for and advised a number of the programmed text publishers (and written my own), discussed *Walden Two* with would-be community founders, evaluated behavior modification projects in the schools, and from time to time amiably exchanged views with Fred Skinner. We come now to his latest and best known work.

I think everyone should have a hobby or two for his days of retirement, and I am delighted that Skinner should have chosen philosophy as one of his. Moreover, as an amateur, he does as well as many professionals in what is indeed a pretty sloppy field. No more sloppy than psychology, in reality, nor education, but the sloppiness is more pervasive and hence more disquieting since in philosophy there are essentially *no* givens, no unarguable data. The solipsist is just as much a member of the club as the realist. But this is as much the strength of philosophy as its weakness, for it is just this property that ensures that *all* the really fundamental disputes remain within philosophy. There is nowhere else for them to go. Physics has that special position in the natural sciences—as does psychology in the behavioral sciences —but philosophy has it in the whole structure of knowledge including physics and psychology.

Philosophy has thus a monopoly on the ultimate issues: they cannot be swept under the well-knit rug of a nearby science, and they are remarkably well-adapted for survival after several millennia of raids by carnivores from the neighboring forests. Their principal adaptive mutation has been slipperiness. Just when the marauder is certain he has them in his jaws, he finds them smiling serenely from beneath a neighboring banyan tree, or vanishing like the Cheshire Cat in that anti-Walden fantasy written by another rather good part-time philosopher, Lewis Carroll (a mathematics don at Oxford who wrote about the philosophy of logic).

Philosophy is very hard to do well, easy to do spectacularly, and impossible to avoid. As a scientist or a citizen you are always making philosophical assumptions, whether you've heard of the subject or not. You take your stand on a moral issue, showing your rejection of moral relativism; you pray, or you do not, showing your views on theism; you try to give up smoking, showing your acceptance of responsibility. And if, like Skinner, you are nervous about making unconsidered assumptions, then you soon find your

---

[1] "A Critique of Radical Behaviorism," in *Minnesota Studies in the Philosophy of Science,* Vol. 1, edited by Feigl and Scriven, University of Minnesota Press, 1956.

way into the field of philosophy to begin your own trophy hunt. Skinner got there before me, and is probably less of an amateur than I am if we look at certification, since I only ever took one course in the subject, and I think he may have taken a couple. So we shall have to settle this one by looking at some arguments rather than diplomas or the roster of allies, since we have none of the first and too many of the second. Of course, the uneasy thing about philosophical arguments is that they are almost never completely conclusive, no doubt contaminated by the slipperiness of the problems with which they have been associated so long. Nevertheless, it is my aim not to let you finish this without conveying to you the power of the alternative position, the hazards of his, and where to go if you wish to look into the matter further. I wish I could undertake to convince you all, but philosophy was not built in a day and a good slice of it comes into this dispute: it cannot be disposed of in an evening.

## OUTLINE

I shall try to support the following sequence of propositions:

A. Skinner's philosophical position is untenable.
B. Skinner's practical-social contributions are valuable.
C. Skinner's philosophical errors may well be responsible for some of his valuable contributions in the practical-social area; but they are neither logically sound bases nor generalizable psychological incentives for such research and applications.
D. Nevertheless, correction of his philosophical errors makes possible, and perhaps probable—even if it does not make certain—considerable progress beyond Skinner's practical-social contributions.
E. It is extremely important that we *do* reject Skinner's philosophy and thereby liberate ourselves and our scientific activities for the next thrust forward, since the costs of continuing with that point of view are rapidly escalating and its pay-off is essentially terminated.

## ON THE UNTENABILITY OF SKINNER'S PHILOSOPHY

There is no short way to deal conclusively with all the issues in *BFD* (*Beyond Freedom and Dignity*, Knopf, 1971). But there is a kind of shock therapy that can break its spell on some of the bewitched, and I shall attempt that here. The book is an attack on the conception of "autonomous man" as defined by Skinner and identified by him with a tradition of naive anti-scientific humanism, by contrast with what he calls the scientific or experimental approach. I now make this assertion: no matter how telling Skinner's arguments are against *some* naive anti-scientific humanists, when they were talking philosophy, nothing that he says significantly affects anything that they said at the practical or social level.

For example, the anti-scientific humanists have said, speaking philosophically, that man is characterized by and should respect freedom and dignity. Skinner gives a bad philosophical argument against this, which we shall examine. But when one gets down to looking at what they meant through investigation of their operational interpretations of it, one finds not only that Skinner is misinterpreting them, but that to a large extent he has the very same views.

What Skinner never realizes, in his overweening commitment to the natural sciences model for psychology, is the extreme epistemological significance of the self-referent nature of psychology. Although thinking that $p$ is true never makes it true when $p$ is a proposition about planets, the opposite is often the case when $p$ is about people. It is obvious to those not blinded by philosophy that there is an important range of antecedent conditions—though by no means the whole and perhaps not even a tenth of that range—over which propositions about performance are true or false accordingly as they are believed or not believed by those to whom they refer. For example, *sometimes some* people are so situated that it's correct to say of them, "If you will *believe* that you can give up smoking for a few days, you *will* give up smoking (at least) for a few days." And some of those people are such that *saying this* to them will lead them (a) to consider it, (b) to accept it, (c) to give up smoking *because* they accepted it, thereby (d) proving that what you said was true. It is entirely appropriate to describe such a person, prior to this interaction, as *capable* of giving up smoking, as *not* being "hopelessly addicted," and hence as possessing a degree of freedom, of autonomy, which he had thought he had lost, and which others have really lost. *That* is what freedom is.

The "literature of freedom," which Skinner attacks as philosophically unsound, is to a large extent, a generalization of this same point. "Workers of the world, unite; you have nothing to lose but your chains," is a proposition whose truth may well appear *only* if it is—substantially—believed, as the unions first argued and then accepted. It is not irrelevant to note that eminent college professors find it very difficult to join unions—I think one reason for this is their dislike of the "subjective" element in situations where "one's thinking makes it so"—especially when the thinking in question has to be group thinking. They are only comfortable with *distance*; their ego-ideal incorporates the idea of *objectivity as separation*, an error *only* in the social sciences, and not seen as one even there if one buys Skinner's philosophy of science, which subsumes them under the paradigm of natural science. It is not surprising that behaviorism has had such support in the social sciences, but it is just too expensive an oversimplification to maintain any longer.

Man's control over his destiny has often sprung from a "blind faith" that he could do something when in fact there was no good evidence that he could. In the absence of that belief, it is highly probable that, in many of these cases, he would *not* have succeeded. The success—embarrassingly— shows that the belief was correct, the believer right. The rational, "objective," scientist was wrong. A better scientist would have seen that this might be one of the cases of a self-verifying belief, a case where a person's or group's fate is really whatever they think it is (as between the two alternatives in question). There's really no reason why an enthusiastic proselytizer for operant conditioning couldn't accept this—it's just a rather odd kind of contingency. But an enthusiast for the *ideology* of operant conditioning is upset by it, because it makes an "inner state" a crucial variable. He desperately tries for a description in terms of earlier contingencies, not seeing that it is *only* another description, not a better one, let alone the true one.

Are these self-affecting cases really significant? They are certainly significant in the history of man, in his political struggles. Perhaps it is a sense of this that has turned off so many of the activists from academic, behavioral social science. Nevertheless, these cases go far beyond the political realm, far beyond the Slaves' Revolt or the Russian Revolution. The most pressing message of the view of *science* found in Koyré-Butterfield-Feyerabend-Conant-Kuhn is that the irrational commitment succeeds—sporadically, but crucially —where no measured "rational" opposition to the prevailing paradigms would have overthrown them. Indeed, if I am right about the poor logical basis for his philosophy of science, Skinner is an excellent example of someone who got things done by transcending the demonstrably reasonable, and what drove him was a vision of how things should be, an inner state if there ever was one. The inescapable fact is that this belief-controllability makes man most unlike planets and atoms. To be more precise, it means that many of man's internal states, those involved in his information-processing and information-acquiring activities, of which he is aware through self-perception of brain states (i.e., by introspection), *dominate* his overt behavior, *explain* it, and even control the truth of *predictions* about his later behavior—and *that* is what sticks in Skinner's craw.

Let me give you some quotations to support the claim that Skinner denies this, and then go on to the question why he slips at this point. The whole error can be summed up in a favorite slogan of his: ". . . no theory changes what it is a theory about; man remains what he has always been" (p. 215). False and reactionary; naive and unscientific to boot. In fact incompatible, not only with evidence about self-fulfilling beliefs, revolutions, etc., but with his own discussions of self-management and the evolution of culture. But let us look at the microstructure of his argument.

He says (*BFD*, p. 42) "Man's struggle for freedom is not due to a will to be free." But *sometimes* it is, and in leaders and those we wish to inspire to leadership, this is quite often and importantly true. The literature of freedom is right: it did not make what Skinner calls "the mistake of defining freedom in terms of states of mind or feelings" (loc. cit.). It *did* emphasize the crucial importance of states of mind, for *sometimes* a free state of mind is exactly what guarantees and effectively constitutes freedom.

Skinner means more by this statement than I have so far discussed. He is involved in another point—a good one —and two other errors. The good point is that a happy slave is still a slave, that objective bonds may not be perceived. We may be unconscious of these bonds because of ignorance or brain washing. But it is certainly an error to suggest that the "literature of freedom" didn't see this point, i.e., that "the literature" has really defined freedom purely subjectively. Where Mill and Leibnitz and Voltaire—the authors he does quote—make such a claim, they are doing so as a clarifying first step, to focus first on *freedom from perceived bonds*, the ones that hurt now. Plenty of other writers have been aware of the "happy slave" problems. In fact, it is the principal argument of the Marxists against free elections in a recently "liberated" country, or in favor of revolution rather than reform in *this* society with its biased media (Marcuse). It is also one of the best arguments against the press censorship typical of most communist countries. This apparent contradiction in practice is related to one in much Marxist literature, which both denies freedom in the name of determinism, and also exhorts the proletariat to strike for freedom. Conflicting *tendencies* in our concept of freedom there certainly are, in Skinner's philosophy as in that of the U.S. Supreme Court's, amongst others; but one cannot represent this as a situation where "the literature of freedom" is introspective and the facts of psychology show it to be wrong.

The most serious weaknesses in Skinner become clear when we examine his alternative to defining freedom in terms of inner states. We should instead—he recommends—define it in terms of arrangements that avoid long-term "exploitative and hence aversive" (p. 40) consequences, such as misery. The authors of the introspectionist definitions of freedom might well sink back with a smile at this point. Skinner has done what he calls rescuing the happy slave who was—he thinks—abandoned by those authors, by arguing that *eventually* the slave won't be happy. If this is true, then eventually *their* supposed definition applies. Since Mill, for example, was a utilitarian, wholly consequence-oriented, he has the best of reasons for changing the exploitative system now—namely, the reason that it will have bad consequences, ones that will be phenomenologically apparent as bad, i.e. misery. So he is in no difficulty at all.

A point in passing; I don't have to tackle in full here Skinner's claim to define "aversive" without reference to sensations, because I'm not making an issue of it. Skinner slides from mentalistic to behavioristic language often enough that I'm not misrepresenting him when I do likewise. (He would of course justify his slides by saying that a feeling like "misery" implies overt aversive responses.) But it *is* interesting to note that his "translations" will work only if the organism is *free to respond,* so that the definition of "aversive" involves—at a first pass—the (or *a*) notion of freedom, which makes it a little awkward to proclaim the reverse (his definition of freedom in terms of aversive responses) as an illuminating analysis.

Behind the scenes of all this discussion of freedom, Skinner is fighting another battle, a battle for the semantic prize of rescuing the word "control" from its generally negative connotations. And in this battle he fights dirty. The scenario goes like this. Skinner: "The literature of freedom has been forced to brand all control as wrong . . . it is unprepared for the next step which is not to free men from control but to analyze and change the kinds of control to which they are exposed" (pp. 42–43).

Incidentally, it's pretty tough on the Marxists to produce a passage of pure Marxist doctrine like that without any acknowledgement to a rather substantial slice of the (admittedly schizophrenic) "literature of freedom" (on *Skinner's* definition of it—p. 30).

Well, a kick in the crotch like that scarcely counts as *real* dirty play. The really dirty play is a barefaced, semantic sneak with the word "control." Skinner does not pull off a profound or scientific re-analysis of the concept. He simply misses the distinction that is built into its normal use.

What he thinks of as an insight is that "the problem is to free men, not from control, but from certain kinds of control" (p. 41), namely "control which does not have aversive sequences at any time" (*ibid.*). What he did not see was that the term "control" *in* the literature of freedom, already incorporates exactly this qualification. Political control, in everyday terms, is something that is *imposed* to *restrict* freedom, i.e. the range of available reinforcing responses. Hence his "insight" is a precise translation of theirs—into a confusing language, confusing because non-standard, and evocative of misleading implications. So the trick is simply this: Skinner first expands the term "control" from its normal usage to cover all cases of behavior responsive to external contingencies. (Of course, from a psychologist's point of view, this makes some sense—but politically it's absurd since control *means* insuperable aversive or damaging conditions.) Then he notices that not all control in this sense is undesirable. Not realizing that he's changed the meaning of the term, he announces this as a discovery. But it's exactly the same point that the politician makes in everyday language when he complains about certain state controls as excessive. One thinks of the hard words of Chomsky's review of the book in the *New York Review of Books* where he suggested that Skinner does nothing but juggle with words.

But the reasons Chomsky gives are quite different from those I have given, and would be unacceptable to almost any behavioral researcher today. I shall return to them later.

It is impossible not to speculate that Skinner's egregious errors in analyzing control may spring from a somewhat unseemly desire to control the world if necessary by semantic fiat, coming as it does from the author of *Walden Two*. Philosophers are often accused of winning points by redefining terms, and by this criterion, Skinner is indeed a philosopher many times over. I have focussed on a few crucial pages—there are a dozen such nodes in the book where one can turn on the highspeed camera, play it back slowly, and see exactly how the rabbit is being brought out of the hat. In each of these cases we do indeed have a little semantic tidying-up to do, and it can be done by a local repair or—absurdly—by insisting on perfection and thus rejecting the whole concept, or building a new one, be it freedom or dignity or control or moral value. With "control" he simply redefines it to cover all non-aversive goal-directed social interaction, which makes one feel delightfully imperial as one passes someone the salt, knowing that he will probably take it. *Thus* we control the world, we feel—the new, scientific, odorfree way.

In the concept of "freedom," on the other hand, he smells a theological rat and, with an equally cavalier gesture, banishes it forever. For no-one is free from control-as-redefined, and that—he says—is what freedom means. No—it means freedom from control-as-*originally*-defined, i.e., free from *aversive* control and that kind of freedom is not only real, but a major goal of his own planned societies.

What about the brain-washed individual, who is *really* controlled, but not aware of it? A serious problem, in fact. But one that is just as serious for him, in translation. And his answer—which is simple—is that the *long-term* consequences of such a system would be aversive. In which case, of course, such an individual would, over the long run, have suffered from control in the usual sense, and hence would not in fact have been free in the usual sense, though at one stage he did not realize this. No problem for the every-day language of the "literature of freedom."

Behind this rejection of freedom as involving lack of control, which—on his definition—makes it impossible, there lies a sub-plot whose scheme is that determinism eliminates freedom, a somewhat different thesis. This comes out most clearly in the totally illicit contrasts he constantly offers the reader. For example, he says, in a passage from which we have so far considered only the first part:

> Man's struggle for freedom is not due to a will to be free, but to certain behavioral processes characteristic of the human organism, the chief effect of which is the avoidance of or escape from so-called "aversive" features of the environment. (P. 42.)

Now it is plausible to suppose that a human reader first attaches meaning to words, then modifies this interpretation in the light of subsequent context, in an effort to divine the writer's or speaker's meaning. Taken in its standard sense, as we have previously discussed it, the categorical denial that freedom is ever due to the will to be free, is simply an empirically false generalization. Then we read on and realize that he intends "will to be free," used as a cause of behavior, to be *incompatible* with behavioral processes involving the presence of aversive stimuli. Since we are (mostly) inclined favorably towards the idea that essentially all behavior is explicable in terms of contingencies of reinforcement and since he makes clear that *he* means the first explanation, the reference to free will, to be *excluded* by the second, we too feel compelled to agree with him in picking the second over the first. This is simply a con job. There is *absolutely* no good reason to take the first to be incompatible with the second, and he's simply wrong to think there is. Certainly he *gives* no plausible reasons to suppose it incompatible. Hence the proper response is not to accept his implicit redefinition of free will as incompatible with contingency explanations and junk its explanatory status; it is to reject the incompatibility and retain both types of explanation. One can explain the fact that a slot machine ejects a bar of chocolate by reference to someone's insertion of a coin *or* by reference to the inner machinery. Neither excludes the other.

The same line of argument I have just used demolishes many other false dilemmas in the book, but we have probably continued long enough to give some credence to my major point, that Skinner's main line of argument is completely fallacious and misleadingly represented.

There is another side to the matter. Skinner says early on: "The text will often seem inconsistent" (p. 23). An external world explanation of this phenomenological event of seeming, is that it *is* inconsistent. Time and again Skinner slips in a way that cannot be patched up. The man who denies the explanatory significance of the will (p. 10 and *passim.*) ends his book with the ringing paens of the planner: man ". . . is indeed controlled by his environment, but we must remember that it is an environment largely of his own making. The evolution of a culture is a gigantic exercise in self-control" (p. 215 and cf. pp. 207–8). Precisely what was there in the literature of freedom or of the naive humanists that was different from this? Really nothing at all—and it is for this reason that I began my critique by saying I would try to show that Skinner's arguments do not count at all against the social and practical content of those against whom he rails. The book is a philosophical shambles—but still as intriguing as astrology is to the untrained mind—and just as far from philosophy or science.

My third thesis was that much of Skinner's contribution may well spring from his philosophical position. To understand how good from errors sometimes comes, it may help to recount an anecdote. I once gave a talk to the graduate colloquium at the University of Minnesota, attended by many psychology graduate students. In the talk I explained how quantum theory and certain classical paradoxes have destroyed the thesis of physical determinism. A professor of psychology came up to me afterwards and attacked me bitterly on the grounds that such talk will undermine the researcher's drive to search for causes. Now, he may be right. It may well be true that one will do better as a scientist in a particular field if one believes what is in fact scientifically false about the whole nature of science. And I think Skinner's passionate methodological commitment to the emptiness of the human organism may well be a major factor in his success in developing devices and management systems that have in my view substantially benefitted education and educational research, as well as drug research (my second thesis). That he does not *actually* believe in the emptiness of the organism is clear enough in this book. ("It would be foolish to deny the existence of that private world. . . . There is an exclusive intimacy about a headache, or heartache . . . ;" p. 191.) Yet his research activities analyzed by a cognitive functionalist would certainly be described as evidencing a commitment to radical behaviorism; and his theoretical works, including this one, have always shown at least some strands of argument which make clear he hankers after, wishes desperately for, the truth of radical behaviorism. If he had come any closer, especially earlier in his career, to believing in the functionality of the conscious mind for psychological explanation and even manipulation, he might well have been caught in a swamp from which he would never have struggled ashore to do good things.

Nevertheless, there is no general moral here. That error leads to good in one man is no grounds for worshipping it in general. It is in fact no reason for becoming even slightly more casual about it. It is only a reason for avoiding fanatical oversimplification about its evil consequences, from treating it like parents treat thier children's involvement with sex or drugs, by grotesque exaggerations that eventually contribute to, instead of prevent, the undesired outcome.

There may have been a budding psychologist or two in that audience in Minneapolis who slackened off a little. But it is a better bet that there were some who avoided butting their heads against a wall in some problem in social psychology or psephology where self-reference destroys determinism. (And a still better bet that no one was affected at all.) It is now almost certain that Einstein's rigidity about indeterminism led to the waste of his later years' research. Our philosophy of science controls our science, indeed. And the best *bet* is the best philosophy of science; Skinner is an exception who only proves the rule that rules about behavior have exceptions.

Let me now turn to a vision of psychology and its philosophy of education and of society that goes beyond Skinner.

## THE GREENING FIELDS BEYOND BEHAVIORISM

I have read about ten major reviews of *BFD* and a few score of letters or papers concerning it. For the most part, I saved that experience until I had completed the preceding sections of this paper. Virtually all were unfavorable, but I do not think that represents the modal judgment of the leading psychologists today. The long hand of behaviorism retains a very firm grip on a very large number of professorial and professional positions, and in reading the critics, it seems unlikely *they* will much affect the hard-headed behaviorist. There is too much petulance, too much careless misreading—Sennett's review in the *New York Times Book Review* is perhaps the worst example of this, since he persisted in his misreading after Skinner's correction of it— and too much simple dogmatism on the other side. I am sure that some of you will feel my own comments have these faults. (But perhaps it will be a *different* group of you that feels this, and then I will have reached some new ones.)

Chomsky's review, in particular, by a man whose intellect, courage, and friendship I value beyond almost all others, is committed to a degree of scepticism about behavioral science that few would share. He says, "At the moment, we have virtually no scientific evidence and not even the germs of an interesting hypothesis about how human behavior is determined" (*New York Review*). I cannot accept that as a fair description of the social sciences, though I am hard to beat in a race for the sceptic's cup. His own views of determinism are so hard to extract from that review that I hesitate to comment on them—yet enough is plain so that I suspect there would not be five votes in his support in a hundred American Educational Research Association members. (Yet parts of his comments are better than any of the others, from *Die Welt* to *New Society*.) I do not think determinism is true. But I think its errors are not the loopholes through which human freedom escapes. Even if it were completely true, freedom would be equally secure. We need a broader field on which to fight than that narrow issue of determinism.

Well, what are the bright pennants with which we should replace the tattered banners of behaviorism? Let me sketch out the coats-of-arms on three such pennants. I fear that in the space available the detail will be slight, but perhaps just enough to convince you that they are more than fantasy.

I shall talk of alternative views of *freedom/autonomy,* of *morality,* and of *scientific method.* Much of what I would say about freedom is implicit in the criticisms I have already made. When Skinner says that the problem is not of whether there will be control, but simply whether there will be good or bad control, he adds nothing to our understanding, because he simply translates the received view into his own terminology. He is there concerned

only with *external* control, control by the environment, by schedules of reinforcement. (Later he comes to talk somewhat of self-control, for example, in
the concluding paragraph of the book, which is quoted above.) I would
want to propose a similar but I hope less trivial treatment of freedom, for I
would say that freedom—in the sense of importance to man—dwells within,
and at harmony with, the constraints of natural and psychological laws.

The crucial question, I would say, is not whether our actions are determined, but whether they are *wholly* determined by *concurrent external*
factors that *override* any variation in mental state—in which case we are not
free—or whether one of the determinants of action (one factor which if
different would make a difference) is a mental state or event, such as pre-
ferring or choosing. Notice that I do not suggest for one moment that the
subject's belief that he is free is decisive. What is decisive is the properties
of the actual causal chain. He may think he is free, though he is not (the
alcoholic, for example); he may think he is not free, though he is (the man
waking from a successful operation to remedy a locked joint). The philosophical charms of determinism will tempt you to say that if his decision or
preference was itself determined, then it is absurd to call him free. But *I* call
him free because he is in fact *capable, able* to do something besides what he
does. You say, how "capable" of doing what is physically guaranteed not to
happen? I reply: look at what "capacity," "ability," "potentiality," really
mean—turn your eyes away from the dazzling glare of the Mad Determinist's
magic, and cast them to the ground again. You will find in your everyday use
the basic sense of those terms, and if you cling firmly to that sense, you will
find the spell has no power over you. For example, it is probably true that
everyone reading this is *capable,* has the *ability* or *capacity* to multiply 17
by 13 in their heads. Supposing that the universe is so set up that the room
in which you sit caves in as soon as you read these words, and you die immediately. Does that refute my claim? Not for one moment. It is true that you
all had that power at the time I claimed it, and the proof is not that you ever
exhibit it, but the evidence that tells us about your education, or more direct
evidence if we could get it, of the state of your brain. Of course, doing it is
excellent evidence for the ability—but not the only kind. You are able to do
many things that you never do, just as a table is able to support weights that
it never will support. Determinism does not destroy, or even bear on, your
capacity to do things which you do not in fact do. Throw off its thrall! And
if you succeed, as a special bonus, I will award you a small medal on which
is engraved the words "Determinism is False Anyway."

The immediate effect of this doctrine on educational research is far more
than you might suppose at first sight. It immediately becomes legitimate to
talk forbidden talk once more; to talk, for example, about the will and the
strength of will in terms of the *amount* of aversive or seductive reinforcement

that it can withstand; and we can begin to discuss again, without embarrassment, the question of *training* the will, of strengthening it. You will notice that I talk of reinforcement again, the language of behaviorism. As a matter of fact, a good deal of recent work on education for self-control has come out of the behavior-modification people, Skinnerians mostly. What I am doing is trying to free them from a verbal taboo that simply confuses their whole perception of what they are trying to do. There is no reason for them not to talk of "building character" and so forth. They are now grown-up enough to be able to discard the policies of *talking* about character improvement to effect real behavior change. They should, he said, rather go out and find the educational *procedures* and *experiences* that will bring about a demonstrable change in behavior, of the kind that produces demonstrable benefits. Skinner's advice was good—but they don't have to say this is *control* and they don't have to deny that the subject is now able to do things of his *own free will* that he couldn't manage before, and they don't have to deny that he does them because he chooses to. In short, we can respect and admire and benefit from Burrhus F. Skinner but we don't have to buy the ideological crap. Like those graduate students, we ought to be mature enough to face up to the falsehood of the philosophical doctrine of determinism without becoming incompetent scientists.

Look at the horror word itself—"autonomy." *BFD* is a polemic against "autonomous man," whose most obvious property is being constituted entirely of straw. I have spent little time on him so far, mainly for that reason. But let me try to show you that the mistaken philosophical objections to autonomy have prevented the Skinnerians from proceeding in directions of the utmost value to us all. One begins with the suspicion that those many writers who have taken the autonomy of the student to be a principal or *the* principal goal of education have not been making a simple logical or scientific mistake, as one would suppose from reading Skinner. Take the following practical problem, typical of many behavior-modification experiments in the classroom (I briefly review most of this literature in the NSSE yearbook cited). We have a classroom in which almost total chaos reigns, in which no noticable learning is occurring, whose teacher is distraught, whose parents are bitter. We discover that setting up a token economy results in intensive learning, an exciting atmosphere for pupils and teacher, gratification for the parents, and so forth. There are just two worries. First, we discover that the use of a substitute teacher, untrained in operating a token economy, immediately leads to disorder again. (And there is no carry-over of positive effect towards learning when these pupils go on to the next grade.) Secondly, and not really independently, some parents begin to worry about introducing a financial motivation for learning—somehow that jars. We have succeeded in developing a supportive system that gets the learning done, but perhaps there are other considerations than efficiency and immediate enjoyment that must be used as criteria in evaluating this innovation.

Clearly the crucial task is to develop in the students what we would normally call an *autonomous* drive for learning or—at the worst—for law and order. There has been some thinking about this on these projects, but not much. If one is mostly interested in behavior and its external conditioners, one is not likely to focus on the inner man. But only the inner man goes home after school, with the student. Only the inner man goes up to the next grade, stays around for the substitute teacher. The reinforcers don't. The experimenter no longer controls the ones that will be there, and they aren't set up to elicit the desired behavior. Not your business, you are inclined to say. Now when I get some behavior-modification-oriented trainers to *focus* on the real problem, they come up with a dozen ingenious and promising suggestions for transfer schedules, re-entry conditioning, etc. I do not believe that the failure of such procedures to have become the great focus in the literature that they are in terms of the problems of education is explicable without reference to the allergy about autonomy.

Consider moral education. Look up the *Handbook of Research on Teaching* or the *Encyclopedia of Educational Research*. What explains the lack of entries? Perhaps the lack of social importance of the subject? Scarcely. The impossibility of success, established by Hartshorne and May 44 years ago? Similar results can be shown for inquiry teaching or problem-solving and a dozen other popular entries. No—it was the positivist legacy that the behaviorist brought to educational research that principally destroyed moral education, and that is as poorly founded as the rejection of autonomy. In fact, there is a very close connection, and it is my fondest hope that in this area particularly one can benefit vastly from throwing off the blinkers of bad philosophy.

One reason for optimism is the extent to which Skinner himself has come to understand the provable value of morality for the society as a whole. There are parts of *BFD* far ahead of anything to come from the positivist-behaviorist camp on morality in its entire history. And yet . . .

And yet he does not see where behaviorism can contribute most. He sees the crucial importance of "doing good for its own sake," of "aiding the society for the sake of the common good," which is what distinguishes morality from mere prudence. He describes ways in which societies have reinforced exactly such behavior. But he cannot make the break with concurrent contingencies. Time after time, he backs away from the obvious necessity, the necessity to *train* ourselves and our children towards an *autonomous* moral drive, one that will work in the absence of any foreseeable reinforcement. It is selfless commitment, not the prudence that he confusedly calls "natural morality," which epitomizes moral behavior as such—and for which the evolutionary advantages are greatest.

It is not *easy* to bring students to the point where they find unselfish acts rewarding. It is a challenge, for a master trainer, an inventive teacher, a behavioral scientist—but Skinner blocks on it, because he cannot *quite* bring himself to the task of modifying the *interior* of the organism in such a way that it will continue to follow a certain behavior pattern *in the absence* of the contingencies that are presently reinforcing for it. To do so is to recognize a further dimension of autonomy in man—his capacity to develop new valences, new sets, new values.

The most recent book on behavior models applied to children, John and Helen Krumboltz' excellent and practical *Changing Children's Behavior,* affords a good example of this shortcoming of the Skinnerians. There is nothing in there, I think it's fair to say, on developing the autonomous drive to respect or help others. Yet there is just about everything else— and the Krumboltz' themselves, kind enough to attend a seminar of mine, were quickly able to suggest a dozen ploys that might work for this crucial bootstrapping step. We must find out whether they will.

Am I not now sounding like the worst bogey of the anti-Skinnerians? brain-washing the kids, out-Skinning Skinner? That is a matter of the gravest concern and we must spend careful professional time on it. Moral education is a moral matter, and if it is indoctrination it may be immoral. Let us legitimate such questions. The forces against value-free social sciences are now overwhelming. Before dying for the cause of empiricism, make sure you read Skinner's argument for the objective validity of morality— not that he'd feel too comfortable with that description and not that I'd feel too happy with some of his logic; but his general line of argument is persuasive there, following his instincts which so often led him in the right direction in these practical matters. Perhaps the philosophical war-cries had to be wrong to attract attention—moderation has always had a bad press. Perhaps the survival value of shocking falsehoods in science today is greater than that of truth. As Skinner would say: if that's true, and as undesirable as it appears, we ought to change the contingencies.

I come at last to the new methodology, and there is no way I can do it justice here. One of the topics I proposed when I was invited to give this associational address, was "A New Epistemology for Educational Research." I decided that was a little too dry to throw at your ears, not the optimal de-coding channel for complex messages. So perhaps it is just as well that I can't stuff it into the toe of the stocking, but I do want you to know that Christmas is coming and that there *are* good things in the stocking. There *is* a new methodology-epistemology that finally kicks off the traces of Newtonian phys-ics. The move to statistics has always had some of that effect, and it is not accidental that Skinner would have none of it. Statistics still has an aura of the second-best about it to those who pine for neat laws and precise prediction. I think I can now see a way to make physics look like a little lucky strike, a way to generalize the notions of knowledge and confirmation and explanation so that we can conceptualize what goes on in educational research without a constant feeling that, even at its best, it can only be an approximation to real science.[2] I think that success in this direction would complete a very satisfactory transcendence of the behaviorist phase in educational research —a phase from which we have learnt a great deal and could never dismiss without loss, one to which we still too often react to by jumping into a hotter fire, but one which we must now come to see in proper perspective, without concessions to its bad philosophy and its imperial disregard of the commonsense insights and distractions embedded in our language.

[2] There are several dimensions in which an adequate methodology for educational research (and for large parts of the social sciences) differs from the traditional one. I have been asked to add some references to this version of the paper that will at least provide hints of the new directions. Kaplan's *The Conduct of Inquiry* often adumbrates them—it's the best single volume reference, but it only goes 10 percent of the way we have to travel. Earlier in this paper I said something about the self-reference feature of the required epistemology. There is more on that in "An Essential Unpredictability in Human Behavior," in *Scientific Psychology*, ed. by Nagel and Wolman (New York: Basic Books, Inc., 1965), 411–25, which shows how determinism fails on classical (i.e., non-quantum) grounds. On the need for a new line between the objective and the subjective, there may be some points of interest in "Objectivity and Subjectivity in Educational Research," in *Yearbook of the National Society for the Study of Education*, 1972. On the new role of explanation and prediction and causation, perhaps the most useful references arise from the study of history, the anti-physics social science, e.g., "Truisms as the Grounds for Historical Explanations," in *Theories of History*, ed. by P. L. Gardiner (New York: Free Press, 1959), 443–75; to these add "The Logic of Cause," in *Theory and Decision,* vol. II, no. 1, October 1971, 49–66 (partly reprinted in *Explanations,* ed. by Gwynn Netter (New York: McGraw-Hill, 1970).

With respect to the role of paradigms in general, there are some reflections in "Psychology without a Paradigm," in *Clinical-Cognitive Psychology,* ed. by Louis Breger, (Englewood Cliffs, N.J.: Prentice-Hall, 1969), 9–24. Few of these discuss the values issue, perhaps the most important new dimension; I can only give an early reference to this, which appears in *Value Claims in the Social Sciences,* Social Science Education Consortium, Boulder, Colorado, 1966. All of this needs tying together, and the way to do it is, in my view, through redoing information theory. I have done this, but the only publication on it is "The Concept of Comprehension; from Semantics to Software," in *Language Comprehension and the Acquisition of Knowledge,* edited by R. O. Freedle (Scripta Publishing Corp., 1972).

# ◦◦( 3 )◦◦

# Ingredients for
# a Theory of Instruction[1]

RICHARD C. ATKINSON [2]

The term "theory of instruction" has been in widespread use for over a decade and during that time has acquired a fairly specific meaning. By con sensus it denotes a body of theory concerned with optimizing the learning process; stated otherwise, the goal of a theory of instruction is to prescribe the most effective methods for acquiring new information, whether in the form of higher-order concepts or rote facts. Although usage of the term is widespread, there is no agreement on the requirements for a theory of instruction. The literature provides an array of examples ranging from speculative accounts of how children should be taught in the classroom to formal mathematical models specifying precise branching procedures in computer-controlled instruction.[3] Such diversity is healthy; to focus on only one approach would not be productive in the long run. I prefer to use the term "theory of instruction" to encompass both experimental and theoretical

[1] A briefer version of this paper was presented as an invited address at the meetings of the American Educational Research Association, Chicago, April, 1972. This research was sponsored in part by National Science Foundation Grant No. NSF GJ-443X2, by Office of Naval Research Contract No. N00014-67-A-0112-0054, and by the National Institute of Mental Health Grant No. MH-21747.

Richard C. Atkinson, "Ingredients for a Theory of Instruction," also appeared in *The American Psychologist* 27, no. 10 (October 1972), 921–931. Copyright 1972 by the American Psychological Association, and reproduced by permission.

[2] Requests for reprints should be sent to Richard C. Atkinson, Department of Psychology, Stanford University, Stanford, California 94305.

[3] See, for example, Smallwood (1962), Carroll (1963), Hilgard (1964), Bruner (1966), Groen and Atkinson (1966), Crothers and Suppes (1967), Gagné (1970), Seidel and Hunter (1970), Pask and Scott (1971), and Atkinson and Paulson (1972).

research, with the theoretical work ranging from general speculative accounts to specific quantitative models.

The literature on instructional theory is growing at a rapid rate. So much so that, at this point, a significant contribution could be made by someone willing to write a book summarizing and evaluating work in the area. I am reminded here of Hilgard's book, *Theories of Learning*, first published in 1948; it played an important role in the development of learning theory by effectively summarizing alternative approaches and placing them in perspective. A book of this type is needed now in the area of instruction. My intention in this paper is to present an overview of one of the chapters that I would like to see included in such a book; a title for the chapter might be "A Decision-Theoretic Analysis of Instruction." Basically, I shall consider the factors that need to be examined in deriving optimal instructional strategies and then use this analysis to identify the key elements of a theory of instruction.

## A DECISION-THEORETIC ANALYSIS OF INSTRUCTION

The derivation of an optimal strategy requires that the instructional problem be stated in a form amenable to a decision-theoretic analysis. Analyses based on decision theory vary somewhat from field to field, but the same formal elements can be found in most of them. As a starting point it will be useful to identify these elements in a general way, and then relate them to an instructional situation. They are as follows:

1. The possible states of nature.
2. The actions that the decision-maker can take to transform the state of nature.
3. The transformation of the state of nature that results from each action.
4. The cost of each action.
5. The return resulting from each state of nature.

In the context of instruction, these elements divide naturally into three groups. Elements 1 and 3 are concerned with a description of the learning process; elements 4 and 5 specify the cost-benefit dimensions of the problem; and element 2 requires that the instructional actions from which the decision-maker is free to choose be precisely specified.

For the decision problems that arise in instruction, elements 1 and 3 require that a model of the learning process exist. It is usually natural to identify the states of nature with the learning states of the student. Specifying the transformation of the states of nature caused by the actions of the decision-maker is tantamount to constructing a model of learning for the situation under consideration. The learning model will be probabilistic to the extent that the state of learning is imperfectly observable or the transformation of the state of learning that a given instructional action will cause is not completely predictable.

The specification of costs and returns in an instructional situation (elements 4 and 5) tends to be straightforward when examined on a short-term basis, but virtually intractable over the long term. For the short term one can assign costs and returns for the mastery of, say, certain basic reading skills, but sophisticated determinations for the long-term value of these skills to the individual and society are difficult to make. There is an important role for detailed economic analyses of the long-term impact of education, but such studies deal with issues at a more global level than we shall consider here. The present analysis will be limited to those costs and returns directly related to a specific instructional task.

Element 2 is critical in determining the effectiveness of a decision-theory analysis; the nature of this element can be indicated by an example. Suppose we want to design a supplementary set of exercises for an initial reading program that involve both sight-word identification and phonics. Let us assume that two exercise formats have been developed, one for training on sight words, the other for phonics. Given these formats, there are many ways to design an overall program. A variety of optimization problems can be generated by fixing some features of the curriculum and leaving others to be determined in a theoretically optimal manner. For example, it may be desirable to determine how the time available for instruction should be divided between phonics and sight-word recognition, with all other features of the curriculum fixed. A more complicated question would be to determine the optimal ordering of the two types of exercises in addition to the optimal allocation of time. It would be easy to continue generating different optimization problems in this manner. The main point is that varying the set of actions from which the decision-maker is free to choose changes the decision problem, even though the other elements remain the same.

Once these five elements have been specified, the next task is to derive the optimal strategy for the learning model that best describes the situation. If more than one learning model seems reasonable *a priori*, then competing candidates for the optimal strategy can be deduced. When these tasks have been accomplished, an experiment can be designed to determine which strategy is best. There are several possible directions in which to proceed after the initial comparison of strategies, depending on the results of the experiment. If none of the supposedly optimal strategies produces satisfactory results, then further experimental analysis of the assumptions of the underlying learning models is indicated. New issues may arise even if one of the procedures is successful. In the second example that we shall discuss, the successful strategy produces an unusually high error rate during learning, which is contrary to a widely accepted principle of programmed instruction (Skiner, 1968). When anomalies such as this occur, they suggest new lines of experimental inquiry, and often require a reformulation of the learning model.[4]

## CRITERIA FOR A THEORY OF INSTRUCTION

Our discussion to this point can be summarized by listing four criteria that must be satisfied prior to the derivation of an optimal instructional strategy:

1. A model of the learning process.
2. Specification of admissible instructional actions.
3. Specification of instructional objectives.
4. A measurement scale that permits costs to be assigned to each of the instructional actions and payoffs to the achievement of instructional objectives.

If these four elements can be given a precise interpretation then it is generally possible to derive an optimal instructional policy. The solution for an optimal policy is not guaranteed, but in recent years some powerful tools have been developed for discovering optimal or near optimal procedures if they exist.

The four criteria listed above, taken in conjunction with methods for deriving optimal strategies, define either a model of instruction or a theory of instruction. Whether the term "theory" or "model" is used depends on the generality of the applications that can be made. Much of my own work has been concerned with the development of specific models for specific instructional tasks; hopefully, the collection of such models will provide the groundwork for a general theory of instruction.

In terms of the criteria listed above, it is clear that a model or theory of instruction is in fact a special case of what has come to be known in the mathematical and engineering literature as *optimal control theory* or, more simply, *control theory* (Kalman, Falb, and Arbib, 1969). The development of control theory has progressed at a rapid rate both in the United States and abroad, but most of the applications involve engineering or economic systems of one type or another. Precisely the same problems are posed in the area of instruction except that the system to be controlled is the human

---

[4] For a more extensive discussion of some of these points see Atkinson and Paulson (1972), Calfee (1970), Dear *et al.* (1967), Laubsch (1970), and Smallwood (1971).

learner, rather than a machine or group of industries. To the extent that the preceding four elements can be formulated explicitly, methods of control theory can be used in deriving optimal instructional strategies.

To make some of these ideas more precise, we shall consider two examples. One involves a *response-insensitive strategy* and the other a *response-sensitive strategy*. A response-insensitive strategy orders the instructional materials without taking into account the student's responses (except possibly to provide corrective feedback) as he progresses through the curriculum. In contrast, a response-sensitive strategy makes use of the student's response history in its stage-by-stage decisions regarding which curriculum material to present next. Response-insensitive strategies are completely specified in advance and consequently do not require a system capable of branching during an instructional session. Response-sensitive strategies are more complex, but have the greatest promise for producing significant gains for they must be at least as good, if not better, than the comparable response-insensitive strategy.

## OPTIMIZING INSTRUCTION IN INITIAL READING

The first example is based on work concerned with the development of a computer-assisted instruction (CAI) program for teaching reading in the primary grades (Atkinson and Fletcher, 1972). The program provides individualized instruction in reading and is used as a supplement to normal classroom teaching; a given student may spend anywhere from zero to 30 minutes per day at a CAI terminal. For present purposes only one set of results will be considered, where the dependent measure is performance on a standardized reading achievement test administered at the end of the first grade. Using our data a statistical model can be formulated that predicts test performance as a function of the amount of time the student spends on the CAI system. Specifically. let $P_i(t)$ be student $i$'s performance on a reading test administered at the end of first grade, given that he spends time $t$ on the CAI system during the school year. Then within certain limits the following equation holds:

$$P_i(t) = \alpha_i - \beta_i \exp(-\gamma_i t)$$

Depending on a student's particular parameter values, the more time spent on the CAI program the higher the level of achievement at the end of the year. The parameters $\alpha$, $\beta$, and $\gamma$, characterize a given student and vary from one student to the next; $\alpha$ and $(\alpha - \beta)$ are measures of the student's maximal and minimal levels of achievement respectively, and $\gamma$ is a rate of progress measure. These parameters can be estimated from a student's response record obtained during his first hour of CAI. Stated otherwise, data from the first hour of CAI can be used to estimate the parameters $\alpha$, $\beta$, and $\gamma$ for a given student, and then the foregoing equation enables us to predict end-of-year performance as a function of the CAI time allocated to that student.

The optimization problem that arises in this situation is as follows: Let us suppose that a school has budgeted a fixed amount of time $T$ on the CAI system for the school year and must decide how to allocate the time among a class of $n$ first-grade students. Assume, further, that all students have had a preliminary run on the CAI system so that estimates of the parameters $\alpha$, $\beta$, and $\gamma$ have been obtained for each student.

Let $t_i$ be the time allocated to student $i$. Then the goal is to select a vector $(t_1, t_2, \ldots, t_n)$ that optimizes learning. To do this let us check our four criteria for deriving an optimal strategy.

The first criterion is that we have a model of the learning process. The prediction equation for $P_i(t)$ does not offer a very complete account of learning; however, for purposes of this problem the equation suffices as a model of the learning process, giving all of the information that is required. This is an important point to keep in mind: the nature of the specific optimization problem determines the level of complexity that must be represented in the learning model. For some problems the model must provide a relatively complete account of learning in order to derive an optimal strategy, but for other problems a simple descriptive equation of the sort presented above will suffice.

The second criterion requires that the set of admissible instructional actions be specified. For the present case the potential actions are simply all possible vectors $(t_1, t_2, \ldots, t_n)$ such that the $t_i$'s are non-negative and sum to $T$. The only freedom we have as decision-makers in this situation is in the allocation of CAI time to individual students.

The third criterion requires that the instructional objective be specified. There are several objectives that we could choose in this situation. Let us consider four possibilities:

(a) Maximize the mean value of $P$ over the class of students.
(b) Minimize the variance of $P$ over the class of students.
(c) Maximize the number of students who score at grade level at the end of the first year.
(d) Maximize the mean value of $P$ satisfying the constraint that the resulting variance of $P$ is less than or equal to the variance that would have been obtained if no CAI was administered.

Objective (a) maximizes the gain for the class as a whole; (b) aims to reduce differences among students by making the class as homogeneous as possible; (c) is concerned specifically with those students that fall behind grade level; (d) attempts to maximize performance of the whole class but ensures that differences among students are not amplified by CAI. Other instructional objectives can be listed, but these are the ones that seemed most relevant. For expository purposes, let us select (a) as the instructional objective.

The fourth criterion requires that costs be assigned to each of the instructional actions and that payoffs be specified for the instructional objectives. In the present case we assume that the cost of CAI does not depend on how time is allocated among students and that the measurement of payoff is directly proportional to the students' achieved value of $P$.

In terms of our four criteria, the problem of deriving an optimal instructional strategy reduces to maximizing the function

$$\phi(t_1, t_2, \ldots, t_n) = \frac{1}{n} \sum_{i=1}^{n} P_i(t_i)$$

$$= \frac{1}{n} \sum_{i=1}^{n} [a_i - \beta_i \exp(-\gamma_i t_i)]$$

subject to the constraint that

$$\sum_{i=1}^{n} t_i = T$$

and

$$t_i \geq 0.$$

This maximization can be done by using the method of dynamic programming (Bellman, 1961). In order to illustrate the approach, computations were made for a first-grade class where the parameters $\alpha$, $\beta$, and $\gamma$ had been estimated for each student. Employing these estimates, computations were carried out to determine the time allocations that maximized the preceding equation. For the optimal policy the predicted mean performance level of the class, $P$, was 15 percent higher than a policy that allocated time equally to students (i.e., a policy where $t_i = t_j$ for all $i$ and $j$). This gain represents a substantial improvement; the drawback is that the variance of the $P$ scores is roughly 15 percent greater than for the equal-time policy. This means that if we are interested primarily in raising the class average, we must let the rapid learners move ahead and progress far beyond the slow learners.

Although a time allocation that complies with objective (a) did increase overall class performance, the correlated increase in variance leads us to believe that other objectives might be more beneficial. For comparison, time allocations also were computed for objectives (b), (c), and (d). Figure 1 presents the predicted gain in $P$ as a percentage of $P$ for the equal-time policy. Objectives (b) and (c) yield negative gains and so they should since their goal is to reduce variability, which is accomplished by holding back on the rapid learners and giving a lot of attention to the slower ones. The

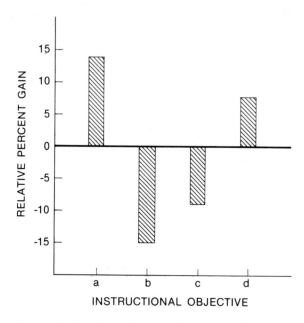

*Figure 1.   Percent gains in the mean value of P when compared with an equal-time policy for four policies each based on a different instructional objective.*

reduction in variability for these two objectives, when compared with the equal-time policy, is 12 percent and 10 percent, respectively. Objective (d), which attempts to strike a balance between objective (a) on the one hand and objectives (b) and (c) on the other, yields an 8 percent increase in P and yet reduces variability by 6 percent.

In view of these computations, objective (d) seems to be preferred; it offers a substantial increase in mean performance while maintaining a low level of variability. As yet, we have not implemented this policy, so only theoretical results can be reported. Nevertheless, these examples yield differences that illustrate the usefulness of this type of analysis. They make it clear that the selection of an instructional objective should not be done in isolation, but should involve a comparative analysis of several alternatives taking into account more than one dimension of performance. For example, even if the principal goal is to maximize P, it would be inappropriate in most educational situations to select a given objective over some other if it yielded only a small average gain while variability mushroomed.

Techniques of the sort presented above have been developed for other aspects of the CAI reading program. One of particular interest involves deciding for each student, on a week-by-week basis, how time should be divided between training in phonics and in sight-word identification (Chant and Atkinson, 1973). However, these developments will not be considered here; it will be more useful to turn to another example of a quite different type.

## OPTIMIZING THE LEARNING OF A SECOND-LANGUAGE VOCABULARY

The second example deals with learning a foreign-language vocabulary. A similar example could be given from our work in initial reading, but this particular example has the advantage of permitting us to introduce the concept of learner-controlled instruction. In developing the example, we will consider first some experimental work comparing three instructional strategies and only later explain the derivation of the optimal strategy.[5]

The goal is to individualize instruction so that the learning of a second-language vocabulary occurs at a maximum rate. The constraints imposed on the task are typical of a school situation. A large set of German-English items are to be learned during an instructional session that involves a series of trials. On each trial one of the German words is presented and the student attempts to give the English translation; the correct translation is then presented for a brief study period. A predetermined number of trials is allocated for the instructional session, and after an intervening period of one week a test is administered over the entire vocabulary. The optimization problem is to formulate a strategy for presenting items during the instructional session so that performance on the delayed test will be maximized.

Three strategies for sequencing the instructional material will be considered. One strategy (designated the random-order strategy) is simply to cycle through the set of items in a random order; this strategy is not expected to be particularly effective but it provides a benchmark against which to evaluate others. A second strategy (designated the learner-controlled strategy) is to let the student determine for himself how best to sequence the material. In this mode the student decides on each trial which item is to be tested and studied; the learner rather than an external controller determines the sequence of instruction. The third scheme (designated the response-sensitive strategy) is based on a decision-theoretic analysis of the instructional task. A mathematical model of learning that has provided an accurate account of vocabulary acquisition in other experiments is assumed to hold in the present situation. This model is used to compute, on a trial-by-trial basis, an individual student's current state of learning. Based on these computations, items are

[5] A detailed account of this research can be found in Atkinson (1972).

selected from trial to trial so as to optimize the level of learning achieved at the termination of the instructional session. The details of this strategy are complicated and can be more meaningfully discussed after the experimental procedure and results have been presented.

Instruction in this experiment is carried out under computer control. The students are required to participate in two sessions: an *instructional session* of approximately two hours and a briefer *delayed-test session* administered one week later. The delayed test is the same for all students and involves a test over the entire vocabulary. The instructional session is more complicated. The vocabulary items are divided into seven lists each containing 12 German words; the lists are arranged in a round-robin order (see Figure 2). On each trial of the instructional session a list is displayed and the student inspects it for a brief period of time. Then one of the items on the displayed list is selected for test and study. In the random-order and response-sensitive conditions the item is selected by the computer. In the learner-controlled condition the item is chosen by the student. After an item has been selected for test, the student attempts to provide a translation; then feedback regarding the correct translation is given. The next trial begins with the computer displaying the next list in the round-robin and the same procedure is repeated. The instructional session continues in this fashion for 336 trials (see Figure 3).

The results of the experiment are summarized in Figure 4. Data are presented on the left side of the figure for performance on successive blocks of trials during the instructional session; on the right side are results from

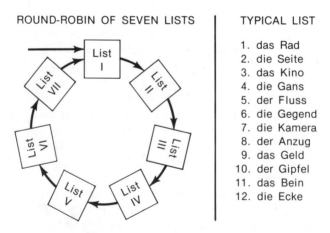

*Figure 2. Schematic representation of the round-robin of display lists and an example of one such list.*

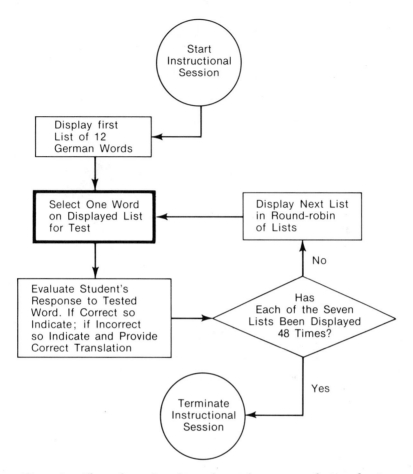

*Figure 3. Flow chart describing the trial sequence during the instruction session. The selection of a word for test on a given trial (box with heavy border) varied over experimental conditions.*

the test session administered one week after the instructional session. Note that during the instructional session the probability of a correct response is highest for the random-order condition, next highest for the learner-controlled condition, and lowest for the response-sensitive condition. The results, however, are reversed on the delayed test. The response-sensitive condition is best by far with 79 percent correct; the learner-controlled condition is next with 58 percent; and the random-order condition is poorest at 38 percent. The observed pattern of results is expected. In the learner-controlled condition

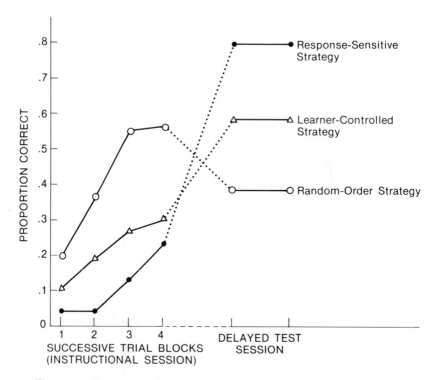

*Figure 4. Proportion of correct responses in successive trial blocks during the instructional session, and on the delayed test administered one week later.*

the students are trying, during the instructional session, to test and study those items they do not know and should have a lower score than students in the random-order condition where testing is random and includes many items already mastered. The response-sensitive procedure also attempts to identify for test and study those items that have not yet been mastered and thus also produces a high error rate during the instructional session. The ordering of groups on the delayed test is reversed since now the entire set of words is tested; when all items are tested the probability of a correct response tells us how much of the list actually has been mastered. The magnitude of the effects observed on the delayed test are large and of practical significance.

Now that the effectiveness of the response-sensitive strategy has been established, let us turn to a discussion of how it was derived. The strategy is based on a model of vocabulary learning that has been investigated in the laboratory and shown to be quite accurate (Atkinson and Crothers, 1964;

Atkinson, 1972). The model assumes that a given item is in one of three states ($P$, $T$, and $U$) at any moment in time. If the item is in state $P$ then its translation is known and this knowledge is "relatively" permanent in the sense that the learning of other vocabulary items will not interfere with it. If the item is in state $T$ then it is also known, but on a "temporary" basis; in state $T$ other items can give rise to interference effects that cause the item to be forgotten. In state $U$ the item is not known and the student is unable to provide a translation. Thus in states $P$ and $T$ a correct translation is given with probability one, whereas in state $U$ the probability is zero.

When a test and study occurs on a given item the following transition matrix describes the possible change in state from the onset of the trial to its termination:

$$\mathbf{A} = \begin{array}{c} P \\ T \\ U \end{array} \begin{array}{ccc} P & T & U \\ \left[\begin{array}{ccc} 1 & 0 & 0 \\ a & 1-a & 0 \\ bc & (1-b)c & 1-c \end{array}\right] \end{array}$$

Rows of the matrix represent the state of the item at the start of the trial and columns its state at the end of the trial. On a trial when some other item is presented for test and study, a transition in the learning state of our original item also may take place; namely, forgetting is possible in the sense that if the item is in state $T$ it may transit into state $U$. This forgetting can occur only if the student makes an error on the other item; in that case the transition matrix applied to the original item is as follows:

$$\mathbf{F} = \begin{array}{c} P \\ T \\ U \end{array} \begin{array}{ccc} P & T & U \\ \left[\begin{array}{ccc} 1 & 0 & 0 \\ 0 & 1-f & f \\ 0 & 0 & 1 \end{array}\right] \end{array}$$

To summarize, consider the application of matrices $\mathbf{A}$ and $\mathbf{F}$ to some specific item on the list; when the item itself is presented for test and study transition matrix $\mathbf{A}$ is applied; when some other item is presented that elicits an error then matrix $\mathbf{F}$ is applied. The foregoing assumptions provide a complete account of the learning process. The parameters in matrices $\mathbf{A}$ and $\mathbf{F}$ measure the difficulty level of a German-English pair and vary across items. On the basis of prior experiments, numerical estimates of these parameters exist for each of the items used in the experiment.

As noted earlier, the formulation of a strategy requires that we be precise about the quantity to be maximized. For the present task, the goal is to maximize the number of items correctly translated on the delayed test. To do this, a theoretical relationship must be specified between the state of learning at the end of the instructional session and performance on the delayed test. The assumption made here is that only those items in state $P$ at the end of the instructional session will be translated correctly on the delayed test; an item in state $T$ is presumed to be forgotten during the intervening week. Thus, the problem of maximizing delayed-test performance involves, at least in theory, maximizing the number of items in state $P$ at the termination of the instructional session.

Having numerical values for parameters and knowing the student's response history, it is possible to estimate his current state of learning.[6] Stated more precisely, the learning model can be used to derive equations and, in turn, compute the probabilities of being in states $P, T,$ and $U$ for each item at the start of trial $n,$ conditionalized on the student's response history up to and including trial $n - 1.$ Given numerical estimates of these probabilities a strategy for optimizing performance is to select that item for presentation (from the current display list) that has the greatest probability of moving into state $P$ if it is tested and studied on the trial. This strategy has been termed the one-stage optimization procedure because it looks ahead one trial in making decisions. The true optimal policy (i.e., an $N$-stage procedure) would consider all possible item-response sequences for the remaining trials and select the next item so as to maximize the number of items in state $P$ at the termination of the instructional session. For the present case the $N$-stage policy cannot be applied because the necessary computations are too time-consuming even for a large computer. Fortunately, Monte Carlo studies indicate that the one-stage policy is a good approximation to the optimal strategy for a variety of Markov learning models; it was for this reason, as well as the relative ease of computing, that the one-stage procedure was employed.[7] The computational procedure described above was implemented on the computer and permitted decisions to be made online for each student on a trial-by-trial basis.

The response-sensitive strategy undoubtedly can be improved upon by elaborating the learning model. Those familiar with developments in learning theory will see a number of ways of introducing more complexity into the model and thereby increasing its precision. We will not pursue such considerations here, however, since our reason for presenting the example was not to theorize about the learning process but rather to demonstrate how a simple learning model can be used to define an instructional procedure.

[6] The student's *response history* is a record (for each trial) of the item presented and the response that occurred. It can be shown that a *sufficient history* exists which contains only the information necessary to estimate the student's current state of learning; the sufficient history is a function of the complete history and the assumed learning model. For the model considered here the sufficient history is fairly simple, but cannot be readily described without extensive notation.

[7] For a discussion of one-stage and $N$-stage policies and Monte Carlo studies comparing them, see Groen and Atkinson (1966), Calfee (1970), and Laubsch (1970).

## CONCLUDING REMARKS

Hopefully, these two examples illustrate the steps involved in developing an optimal strategy for instruction. Both examples deal with relatively simple problems and thus do not indicate the range of developments that have been made or that are clearly possible. It would be a mistake, however, to conclude that this approach offers a solution to the problems facing education. There are some fundamental obstacles that limit the generality of the work.

The major obstacles may be identified in terms of the four criteria we specified as prerequisites for an optimal strategy. The first criterion concerns the formulation of learning models. The models that now exist are totally inadequate to explain the subtle ways by which the human organism stores, processes, and retrieves information. Until we have a much deeper understanding of learning, the identification of truly effective strategies will not be possible. However, an all-inclusive theory of learning is not a prerequisite for the development of optimal procedures. What is needed instead is a model that captures the essential features of that part of the learning process being tapped by a given instructional task. Even models that may be rejected on the basis of laboratory investigation can be useful in deriving instructional strategies. The two learning models considered in this paper are extremely simple, and yet the optimal strategies they generate are quite effective. My own preference is to formulate as complete a learning model as intuition and data will permit and then use that model to investigate optimal procedures; when possible the learning model will be represented in the form of mathematical equations but otherwise as a set of statements in a computer-simulation program. The main point is that the development of a theory of instruction cannot progress if one holds the view that a complete theory of learning is a prerequisite. Rather, advances in learning theory will affect the development of a theory of instruction, and conversely the development of a theory of instruction will influence research on learning.

The second criterion for deriving an optimal strategy requires that admissible instructional actions be clearly specified. The set of potential instructional inputs places a definite limit on the effectiveness of the optimal strategy. In my opinion, powerful instructional strategies must necessarily be adaptive; that is, they must be sensitive on a moment-to-moment basis to a learner's unique response history. My judgment on this matter is based on limited experience, restricted primarily to research on teaching initial reading. In this area, however, the evidence seems to be absolutely clear: the manipulation of method variables accounts for only a small percentage of the variance when not accompanied by instructional strategies that permit individualization. Method variables like the modified teaching alphabet, oral reading, the linguistic approach, and others undoubtedly have beneficial effects. However, these effects are minimal in comparison to the impact that is possible when instruction is adaptive to the individual learner. Significant progress in dealing with the nation's problem of teaching reading will require individually prescribed programs, and sophisticated programs will necessitate some degree of computer intervention either in the form of CAI or computer-managed instruction. As a corollary to this point, it is evident from observations of students on our CAI Reading Program that the more effective the adaptive strategy the less important are extrinsic motivators. Motivation is a variable in any form of learning, but when the instructional process is truly adaptive the student's progress is sufficient reward in its own right.

The third criterion for an optimal strategy deals with instructional objectives, and the fourth with cost-benefit measures. In the analyses presented here, it was tacitly assumed that the curriculum material being taught is sufficiently beneficial to justify allocating time to it. Further, in both examples the costs of instruction were assumed to be the same for all strategies. If the costs of instruction are equal for all strategies, they may be ignored and attention focused on the comparative benefits of the strategies. This is an important point because it greatly simplifies the analysis. If both costs and benefits are significant variables, then it is essential that both be accurately estimated. This is often difficult to do. When one of these quantities can be ignored, it suffices if the other can be assessed accurately enough to order the possible outcomes. As a rule, both costs and benefits must be weighed in the analysis, and frequently subtopics within a curriculum vary significantly in their importance. In some cases, whether or not a certain topic should be taught at all is the critical question. Smallwood (1971) has treated problems similar to the ones considered in this article in a way that includes some of these factors in the structure of costs and benefits.

My last remarks deal with the issue of learner-controlled instruction. One way to avoid the challenge and responsibility of developing a theory of instruction is to adopt the view that the learner is the best judge of what to study, when to study, and how to study. I am alarmed by the number of individuals who advocate this position despite a great deal of negative evidence. Don't misinterpret this remark. There obviously is a place for the learner's judgments in making instructional decisions. In several CAI programs that I have helped develop, the learner plays an important role in determining the path to be followed through the curriculum. However, using the learner's judgment as one of several items of information in making an instructional decision is quite different from proposing that the learner should have complete control. Our data, and the data of others, indicate that the learner is not a particularly effective decision-maker. Arguments against learner-controlled programs are unpopular in the present climate of opinion, but they need to be made so that we will not be seduced by the easy answer that a theory of instruction is not required because, "who can be a better judge of what is best for the student than the student himself."

The aim of this paper was to illustrate the steps involved in deriving an optimal strategy and their implications for a theory of instruction. I want to emphasize a point made at the outset—namely, that the approach is only one of many that needs to be pursued. Obviously the main obstacle is that adequate theories as yet do not exist for the learning processes that we most want to optimize. However, as the examples indicate, analyses based on highly simplified models can be useful in identifying problems and focusing research efforts. It seems clear that this type of research is a necessary component in a program designed to develop a general theory of instruction.

## REFERENCES

Atkinson, R. C. Optimizing the learning of a second-language vocabulary. *Journal of Experimental Psychology*, 1972, 96, 124–129.

———, and Crothers, E. J. A comparison of paired-associate learning models having different acquisition and retention axioms. *Journal of Mathematical Psychology*, 1964, 1, 285–315.

———, and Fletcher, J. D. Teaching children to read with a computer. *The Reading Teacher*, 1972, 25, 319–327.

———, and Paulson, J. A. An approach to the psychology of instruction. *Psychological Bulletin*, 1972, in press.

Bellman, R. *Adaptive control processes*. Princeton, N. J.: Princeton University Press, 1961.

Bruner, J. S. *Toward a theory of instruction*. Cambridge, Mass.: Harvard University Press, 1966.

Calfee, R. C. The role of mathematical models in optimizing instruction. *Scientia: Revue Internationale de Synthèse Scientifique*, 1970, 105, 1–25.

Carroll, J. B. A model of school learning. *Teachers College Record*, 1963, 64, 723–733.

Chant, V. G., and Atkinson, R. C. Optimal allocation of instructional effort to interrelated learning strands. *Journal of Mathematical Psychology*, 1973, in press.

Crothers, E. J., and Suppes, P. *Experiments in second-langauge learning*. New York: Academic Press, 1967.

Dear, R. E., Silberman, H. F., Estavan, D. P., and Atkinson, R. C. An optimal strategy for the presentation of paired-associate items. *Behavioral Science,* 1967, *12,* 1–13.

Gagné, R. M. *The conditions of learning.* (2nd ed.) New York: Holt, Rinehart & Winston, 1970.

Groen, G. J., and Atkinson, R. C. Models for optimizing the learning process. *Psychological Bulletin,* 1966, *66,* 309–320.

Hilgard, E. R. *Theories of learning.* New York: Appleton-Century-Crofts, 1948.

———— (Ed.). Theories of learning and instruction. In *Sixty-third Yearbook of the National Society for the Study of Education.* Chicago: The University of Chicago Press, 1964.

Kalman, R. E., Falb, P. L., and Arbib, M. A. *Topics in mathematical system theory.* New York: McGraw-Hill, 1969.

Laubsch, J. H. Optimal item allocation in computer-assisted instruction. *IAG Journal,* 1970, *3,* 295–311.

Pask, G., and Scott, B. C. E. Learning and teaching strategies in a transformational skill. *British Journal of Mathematical and Statistical Psychology,* 1971, *24,* 205–229.

Seidel, R. J., and Hunter, H. G. The application of theoretical factors in teaching problem-solving by programed instruction. *International Review of Applied Psychology,* 1970, *19,* 41–81.

Skinner, B. F. *The technology of teaching.* New York: Appleton-Century-Crofts, 1968.

Smallwood, R. D. *A decision structure for teaching machines.* Cambridge, Mass.: MIT Press, 1962.

————. The analysis of economic teaching strategies for a simple learning model. *Journal of Mathematical Psychology,* 1971, *8,* 285–301.

# ❧ 4 ❧

# Individuals and Learning:
# The New Aptitudes [1]

## ROBERT GLASER

In this paper, I propose to show how certain developments in psychology have influenced present educational methods, and to show further how recent work in learning theory, developmental psychology, and psychometrics strongly suggests new directions for educational research and practice. I shall discuss this theme in the context of a central problem in education—the individualization of instruction or, in other terms, adapting educational environments to individual differences. I shall focus on the education of the young child in the preschool and elementary school years, although what I have to say seems applicable to all levels of our educational system. The problem obviously has been a persistent one; it has been recognized and proclaimed at least since the beginning of this century, three generations ago. Very early in the century, Edward L. Thorndike (1911) published a monograph entitled "Individuality." His editor's introduction summarizes the then current situation by noting that the teaching profession and education in general were showing signs of a violent reaction against the uniformity of method that for so long clutched and mechanized the schools. The deadening effects of uniformity needed to be recognized. Parents and students had been the first to notice this; now the professional consciousness was deeply penetrated because the teachers

[1] Presidential Address, American Educational Research Association, Chicago, April, 1972. The preparation of this paper was carried out under the auspices of the Learning Research and Development Center at the University of Pittsburgh, supported in part by funds from the United States Office of Education, Department of Health, Education, and Welfare. This chapter has also appeared in *The Educational Researcher* 1, no. 6 (June, 1972), 5–13.

83

themselves realized that they were caught in the iron machinery of their own making. These turns of phrase were written in 1911, and throughout the twentieth century, the problem has been raised again and again. In 1925, a major effort appeared in the Twenty-fourth Yearbook of the National Society for the Study of Education entitled *Adapting the Schools to Individual Differences.* Carleton Washburne's introduction states in forceful terms that the widespread use of intelligence and achievement tests has made every educator realize that children vary greatly as individuals, and "throughout the educational world, there has therefore awakened the desire to find some way of adapting schools to the differing individuals who attend them [Washburne, 1925]."

Shouts of alarm have been ubiquitous; many suggestions have been made, and a few sustained experiments have been launched. Nevertheless, it is now 1972, and time goes by with still only a recognition of the problem, but as yet, no directions towards solution realized. This is the situation that I would like to examine. I am encouraged to do so by the fact that work in the study of human behavior over the past ten to 20 years now points to possible solutions. Unfortunately, I cannot point to new directions in a simple way by listing a few principles that ring with self-evident truth, although this is the fashionable road to current educational reform. The story is complicated, its roots are deep, and its complexities need to be examined.

## SELECTIVE AND ADAPTIVE MODES OF EDUCATION

An analysis of the problem involves the idiosyncracies of two major fields of psychology. As is known, the English and German traditions of the nineteenth century gave rise to two separate disciplines of scientific psychology: psychometrics and experimental psychology. It was the psychometricians with their emphasis on technology who had significant impact upon educational methods. Indeed, the major activity in educational psychology revolved around measurement and psychometric practice. Psychometrics emphasized the nature of individual differences and the utility of measuring these differences for education. Learning variables and modification of the educational environment, however, were not part of this field. Meanwhile, the experimental psychologists went into the laboratory to work on the basic foundations of their science, and concentrated on discovering and formulating general laws of behavior unencumbered by the additional complication of individual differences. For the most part, individual differences became the error variance in experimental design.

The separation of these two fields, both of which are necessary for a complete conception of instructional theory, led to assumptions about individual differences uninfluenced by knowledge of learning and cognitive processes, and led to theories of learning uninfluenced by the effect of individual difference parameters. In this climate, characterized by the parallel, but not combined, labors of two major disciplines relevant to education, the search for an educational system that responds to individuality has been going on. To be as clear as I can, I will overstate the case by contrasting two kinds of educational environments. One I shall call a selective educational mode, and the other, an adaptive educational mode. It appears that we have produced a selective educational mode while aspiring toward an adaptive one.

A *selective* mode of education is characterized by minimal variation in the conditions under which individuals are expected to learn. A narrow range of instructional options is provided, and a limited number of ways to succeed are available. Consequently, the adaptability of the system to the student is limited, and alternative paths that can be selected for students with different backgrounds and talents are restricted. In such an environment, the fixed or limited paths available require particular student abilities, and these *particular* abilities are emphasized and fostered to the exclusion of other abilities. In this sense, the system becomes selective with respect to individuals who have particular abilities for success—as success is defined and as it can be attained by the means of instruction that are available. The effectiveness of the system, for the designers of the system and for the students themselves, is enhanced by admitting only those students who score very highly on measures of the abilities required to succeed. Furthermore, since only those students who have a reasonable probability of success are admitted, little change in the educational environment is necessary, and the differences among individuals that become important to measure are those that predict success in this special setting.

In contrast to a selective mode, an *adaptive* mode of education assumes that the educational environment can provide for a wide range and variety of instructional methods and opportunities for success. Alternate means of learning are adaptive to and are in some way matched to knowledge about each individual—his background, talents, interests, and the nature of his past performance. An individual's styles and abilities are assessed either upon entrance or during the course of learning, and certain educational paths are elected or assigned. Further information is obtained about the learner as learning proceeds, and this, in turn, is related to subsequent alternate learning opportunities. The interaction between performance and the subsequent nature of the educational setting is the defining characteristic of an adaptive mode. The success of this adaptive interaction is determined by the extent to which the student experiences a match between his specific abilities and interests, and the activities in which he engages. The effect of any election of or assignment to an instructional path is evaluated by the changes it brings about in the student's potential for future learning and goal attainment. Measures of individual differences in an adaptive educational mode are valid to the extent that they help to define alternate paths that result in optimizing immediate learning, as well as long-term success.

A selective educational mode operates in a Darwinian framework, requiring that organisms adapt to, and survive in, the world as it is; an alternative is that the environment can be changed. If we design only a relatively fixed environment, then a wide range of background capabilities and talented accomplishments might be lost from view because of the exclusive reliance upon selection for survival in a particular setting. What is learned and the way in which one learns, and learns to learn, may take on less importance or receive less emphasis in a setting that offers more options for learning.

When one compares a selective educational mode with adaptive educational possibilities, one asks whether the particular selective tests and sorting out devices that are part of present schooling fail to consider abilities and talents that might emerge as important in a more interactive setting where there is room for adjustment between abilities and modes of learning. In principle, and in contrast to traditional practice, there seems to be no reason why educational environments cannot be designed to accommodate more readily to variations in the backgrounds, cognitive processes, interests, styles, and other requirements of learners.

In any educational mode, then, the individual differences that take on outstanding importance have ecological validity within a particular system. In our traditional selective educational mode, the individual differences that are measured in order to make educational assignments center around the concepts of intelligence and aptitude. This bears looking into.

## INTELLIGENCE, APTITUDES, AND LEARNING

Of the various attempts to measure intellectual ability that began at the turn of the century, Binet's work emerged strongly. It was a practical endeavor to predict school success. The Minister of Public Education in France supported Binet's attempts to determine what might be done to ensure the benefits of instruction to retarded children. It was decided that children suspected of retardation be given an examination to certify that, because of the state of their intelligence, they were unable to profit from instruction as given in ordinary schooling. Scholastic success in an essentially fixed educational mode was the predictive aim toward which this test was directed, for which its items were selected, and in terms of which its overall effectiveness was validated; although to be fair to Binet, his writings do indicate a great deal of sensitivity to the possibilities for individual differential diagnosis. Nevertheless, the validation of a test is a very specific procedure in which individuals are exposed to particular kinds of test items that are constructed to predict a particular criterion measure. No test is simply valid in general, but for a specific purpose and a particular situation. The concept of Binet's work has persisted, and as Cronbach points out in the 1970 edition of his well-known book on the essentials of psychological testing: "Current tests differ from those of the earlier generation just as 1970 automobiles differ from those of about 1920: more efficient, more elegant, but operating on the same principles as before [Cronbach, 1970, p. 144]."

At the present time, our most respected textbooks on the subject (Cronbach, 1970; Tyler, 1965) carefully point out that if we base our conclusions about what intelligence tests measure on their most effective use—that is, their predictive validity—then the verdict is that they are tests of scholastic aptitude or scholastic ability; these tests measure certain abilities that are helpful in most school work, as it is conducted in present-day school situations. This same ideology has penetrated the entrance requirements of almost all institutions of higher education (see Wing and Wallach, 1971), and strongly determines the character of primary and secondary school education. It is further to be observed that these tests of scholastic aptitude, when considered over all school levels, account for only 35 to 45 percent of the variation in school performance.

Being aware of this, we have not been remiss in attempting to probe deeper into the different facets of human behavior that might allow us to be more sensitive to individual differences. Some years ago, as a result of some dissatisfaction with the research on the IQ and together with the results of work on multiple factor analysis, there was a deemphasis of the concept of general intelligence that led to the popularity of tests of differential aptitudes. At that time, in addition to an overall measure of "intelligence" or "general aptitude," schools began to employ tests that provided measures on a variety of factors such as spatial, mechanical, and abstract reasoning aptitudes. More than predicting overall scholastic success, these test batteries attempted to predict differential success in school programs leading to different vocations which appeared to require different aptitude patterns.

In 1964, a careful analysis was done by McNemar of the validity coefficients of certain widely used, multi-test differential aptitude batteries. He argued from his analysis that "aside from tests of numerical ability having differential value for predicting school grades in math, it seems safe to conclude that the worth of the multi-test batteries as differential predictors of achievement in school has not been demonstrated [McNemar, 1964]." McNemar further concluded that "it is far from clear that tests of general intelligence have been outmoded by the multi-test batteries as the more useful predictors of school achievement." In general, a simple, unweighted combination of tests of verbal reasoning and numerical ability predicted grades as well as, or better than, any other test or combination of more specific ability tests; and these tests of verbal and numerical ability were similar to what was measured in group tests of intelligence. More recent evidence reaffirms McNemar's conclusion. For example, a 1971 technical report of the College Entrance Examination Board points out that there is certainly no reason why the Scholastic Aptitude Test (SAT) could not include measures from other domains in addition to the verbal and mathematical skills tested, and that research to identify these other domains has been an enduring concern. Yet, over the 40 years of the SAT's existence, no other measures have demonstrated such a broadly useful relationship to the criterion of college achievement (Angoff, 1971).

All this suggests the following observation: Given the characteristics of our present educational system, certain general measures of the ability to manipulate numbers and words predict, to a limited extent, the ability to emerge victorious from the educational environment provided. However, any attempt to further differentiate specific ability patterns that relate to specific educational programs is, at best, no more successful than the usual general ability measures or intelligence measures. Why is this so, and what does it mean?

One clue to answering this question is to note that tests of general ability, intelligence, and aptitude follow the accepted practice of attempting to predict the *outcomes* of learning in our rather uniform educational programs. These tests make little attempt to measure those abilities that are related to different *ways* of learning. The generally used scholastic aptitude tests are designed for and validated in terms of predictions of the products of learning in a particular setting. They are not designed to determine the different ways in which different students learn best, to measure the basic processes that underlie various kinds of learning, nor to assess prerequisite performance capabilities required for learning a new task.

Psychologists and educational researchers, again, have not been insensitive to this state of affairs, and there has been a recent emergence of concern about the relationships between measures of individual differences and learning variables. To a large extent, this work was heralded by the 1957 book by Cronbach and Gleser entitled *Psychological Tests and Personnel Decisions* and its second edition in 1965. This book was concerned with the development of a decision-theory model for the selection and placement of individuals into various "treatments." The word treatment was given a broad meaning, referring to what is done with an individual in an institutional setting; e.g., for what job an applicant should be trained in industry, to what therapeutic method a patient should be assigned, and in education, to which particular educational program or instructional method a student should be assigned or given the opportunity to select. This theoretical analysis attempted to show that neither the traditional predictive model of psychometric work nor the traditional experimental comparison of mean differences was an adequate formulation for these practical decisions, including the kinds of decisions required for the individualization of instruction.

Cronbach and Gleser pointed out that aptitude information is useful in adapting to treatments only when aptitude and treatment can be shown to interact. In a nontechnical way, this can be explained as follows: Given a measure of aptitude, and two different instructional methods, if the aptitude measure correlates positively with success in both treatments, then it is of no value in deciding which method to suggest to the student. What is required is a measure of aptitude that predicts who will learn better from one curriculum or method of learning than from another. If such measures can be developed, then methods of instruction can be designed, not to fit the average person, but to fit an individual or groups of students with particular aptitude patterns. Unless one treatment is clearly best for everyone, treatments should be differentiated in such a way as to maximize their interaction with aptitude variables.

Following up on this logic, educational psychologists have been active in experimentation and have searched deeply into the literature of their field. The line of investigation has been called the ATI problem (ATI standing for aptitude-treatment interaction). The intent of the work is different from that of the previously mentioned work on differential aptitude testing. In the differential aptitude testing research, emphasis was placed on determining the relationship between measured aptitudes and learning outcomes under relatively fixed educational programs. In the ATI work, the emphasis is on determining whether aptitudes can predict which one of several learning methods might help different individuals attain similar educational outcomes. To be clearer, the earlier differential aptitude work assumed several different educational programs, each one leading to different careers, and attempted to select individuals with respect to their potential success in each program. The ATI work essentially assumes that if within each of these several programs there were different instructional options, then aptitude patterns might predict the option in which a student would be most successful.

Several recent comprehensive reviews report detailed analyses of ATI studies (Bracht, 1969; Bracht and Glass, 1968; Cronbach and Snow, 1969). In a review by Bracht, 90 studies were each carefully assessed for the significance of appropriate aptitude-treatment interactions. The results of his survey are quite striking. In the 90 studies, 108 individual difference-treatment interactions were examined; of these, only five were identified as being significant with respect to the kind of interaction required for the purposes I have outlined. An extensive and thoughtful analysis of many of the ramifications of the ATI problem also has appeared in an informal report by Cronbach and Snow (1969). The report is far ranging, discussing the relationships between individual differences and learning from many points of view. Their conclusion, with respect to ATI research, is similar to Bracht's: few or no ATI effects have been solidly demonstrated; the frequency of studies in which appropriate interactions have been found is low; and the empirical evidence found in favor of such interactions is often not very convincing.

This is an astounding conclusion; it implies that our generally used aptitude constructs are not productive dimensions for measuring those individual differences that interact with different ways of learning. These measures, derived from a psychometric, selection-oriented tradition, do not appear to relate to the processes of learning and performance that have been under investigation in experimental and developmental psychology. The treatments investigated in the ATI studies were not generated by any systematic analysis of the kinds of psychological processes called upon in particular instructional methods, and individual differences were not assessed in terms of these processes.

Perhaps we should have known all this, and not have had to learn it the hard way, because I am reminded of Lee Cronbach's APA presidential address of 1957. In discussing these general concerns, he said: "I believe that we will find these aptitudes to be quite unlike our present aptitude measures." He went on to say, "Constructs originating in differential psychology are now being tied to experimental variables. As a result, the whole theoretical picture in such an area as human abilities is changing [Cronbach, 1957]." I believe that Cronbach was a moment or two ahead of his time in his address 15 years ago. But, I also believe that education and psychology have since moved in directions which make adaptation to individuals in educational settings more likely; research on cognitive processes, psychometric methodologies, deeper attempts at individualization, and the cultural Zeitgeist seem to offer enabling potentials. I shall go on to describe some of this, but first let me recapitulate the question that I am attempting to answer.

The general question takes the form of the following set of questions: (1) How can knowledge of an individual's patterns of abilities and interests be matched to the method, content, and timing of his instruction? (2) How can the educational environment be adjusted to an individual's particular talents, and to his particular strengths and weaknesses as defined in terms of social and personal objectives for education? and (3) The other way around—how can an individual's abilities be modified and strengthened to meet the prerequisite demands of available means of instruction and available educational opportunities?

## COGNITIVE PERFORMANCE
## AND INDIVIDUAL DIFFERENCES

The implications of my discussion so far appear to support the hypothesis that the human performances that we identify with the words "general ability," "scholastic intelligence," and "aptitudes" have emerged on the basis of measurement and validation procedures in an educational system of a particular kind. These intelligence and aptitude factors have taken on significance because of their correlation with instructional outcomes, and not because of their relationship to learning processes or different educational techniques. Furthermore, since our educational system provides a limited range of educational options for adapting to different individuals, these general abilities override the influence of any more specific abilities that might be additionally useful if alternate ways of learning were available.

The question now is: What *are* these "new aptitudes"? Current lines of research indicate that a fruitful approach is the conceptualization of individual difference variables in terms of the process constructs of contemporary theories of learning, development, and human performance. There is ample evidence to show that we can experimentally identify and influence a variety of cognitive processes that are involved in new learning, and it appears that the analysis of individual differences in performance can be carried out in terms of such processes (Melton, 1967). Some exemplary studies along these lines can be referred to as illustration. For example, it is known that learning to remember a list of words takes place more effectively when the learner is provided with, or provides for himself, some visual or verbal relationship between pairs of words. Presented with the words "boy" and "horse," one pictures a boy riding a horse, or makes up a sentence containing these words. This process has been called "mental elaboration," referring to the fact that individuals recode or transform materials presented to them by elaborating the content. William Rohwer has been particularly concerned with studying the developmental and individual difference aspects of this process. As children grow older, they begin to generate their own forms of mental elaboration; young children, however, profit from being prompted or encouraged in some way to engage in elaborative activity. Rohwer's work suggests that individual differences, related to children's backgrounds, influence the way in which they carry out cognitive processes of this kind. He further implies that since this kind of elaborative activity facilitates learning in general, it would be fruitful to train particular children in such elaborative techniques of learning; there is evidence that this indeed can be done to extend the capabilities of young learners (Rohwer, 1970a, 1970b, 1971).

In another series of studies related to our work on individualized instruction at Pittsburgh, my colleague Jerome Rosner has studied perceptual processes that appear to be related to basic academic tasks in elementary school. He has studied individual differences in visual and auditory perceptual processes concerned with competence in organizing and extracting patterns of information presented in geometric patterns and in sound combinations. Rosner's work indicates that competence in these processes is differentially related to academic achievement in arithmetic and reading; visual perceptual processes are more related to arithmetic than reading, and auditory processes more related to beginning reading than arithmetic. He has also shown that these processes themselves can be effectively taught to children, and the indication is that the effects of this instruction transfer to specific accomplishment in the beginnings of verbal and quantitative literacy (Rosner, 1972).

Studies such as these support the promise of a line of research on individual differences in terms of cognitive processes. I would urge that studies attempt to identify the kinds of processes required by various tasks, and to characterize how individuals perform these processes. The conditions required to learn the task could then be adapted to these individual characteristics, or the individual might be taught how to engage more effectively in these processes.

Another sign of support for the theme of process concepts as individual difference variables comes from the work on cognitive styles or personality characteristics that influence learning and performance (Kagan and Kogan, 1970). Here, the influence of individual differences in non-cognitive domains on the cognitive processes involved in problem-solving is being systematically studied. This includes research on the effects of cultural background on the dominance of visual, auditory, or tactile sense modalities; the relationship between anxiety and the quality of immediate memory; the ability to hold changing images in memory, what personality theorists have called "leveling and sharpening"; and the degree to which an individual pauses to evaluate the quality of cognitive products in the course of problem-solving, generally referred to as differences in reflection and impulsivity.

There have been some interesting attempts to modify cognitive style. For example, it has been shown that when first-grade children are placed with experienced teachers who have a reflective style, the children become more reflective during the school year than children who are placed with impulsive teachers (Yando and Kagan, 1968). The practical implication of this for school instruction is tailoring the tempo of the teacher to the tempo of the child so that, for example, the behavior of the impulsive child is influenced by the presence of a reflective teacher model. Another set of studies has investigated the controlling function of covert speech as a self-guidance procedure whereby impulsive children are taught to talk to themselves in order to modify their problem-solving styles (Meichenbaum, 1971; Meichenbaum and Goodman, 1969).

The processes that make up cognitive style are important to consider in the education of culturally disadvantaged children. As we know, early experience in a particular cultural environment provides the child with a set of values and a set of techniques and skills for learning to learn and for processing incoming information. It has been pointed out that the middle-class child acquires these things so that they are continuous with what will be required of him in school. Whereas, what a lower socioeconomic-class child acquires may be discontinuous with what school demands. In a non-adaptive environment for learning, "cultural deprivation" is defined in terms of a set of experiences that establishes a discontinuity between preschool experiences and school requirements. An obvious example in the conventional school is that, explicitly or implicitly, the school requires the immediate acceptance of an achievement ethic with deferred future rewards, a characteristic most consonant with middle-class values. This discontinuity has a profound effect on the child's behavior towards school and on the school's behavior toward the child. In the adaptive educational environment that I envision, it would be assumed as a matter of course that the values, styles, and learning processes that the child brings to school are of intrinsic worth. These modes of behavior have, in fact, been extremely functional in the child's environment, and an adaptive setting would work with these assets of the child's functioning as a basis for a program of education (Getzels, 1966).

The work and theories of Piaget quite directly support and influence my theme of the importance of modifiable behavioral processes in adaptive education as opposed to notions of relatively fixed intelligence and aptitude. The stages of cognitive development described in the Piagetian theory of intelligence are thought to mark major qualitative changes in the modes of thinking available to the child and, consequently, changes in the kinds of specific learning of which he or she is capable. Adaptive education, as I have indicated, looks at this in two ways: the educational environment accommodates to the existing modes and processes of a learner, and it also can influence these processes through instruction. The stages described by Piaget thus provide individual modes of performance available to different children which would have to be considered in educational design.

Recently, Lauren Resnick and I (1972) carried out a detailed survey on the possible teachability of basic aptitudes and Piagetian processes. In our examination of operational thinking, particularly the acquisition of concrete operations, with which most studies have been concerned, we noted a significant shift, as compared with a few years ago, in the balance of evidence concerning the trainability of these processes. A number of studies have appeared which offer grounds for suggesting the possibility of developing operational thinking through instruction. As we completed this survey, we were struck with the fact that our search for work on the instructability of basic abilities uncovered far fewer studies on the training of psychometrically defined aptitudes and abilities than on the training of Piagetian and related concepts. This raises the question of why the Piagetian definition of intelligence has stimulated so much more instructional research than has the psychometric one.

One answer seems to be that Piagetian theory is not concerned with differential prediction, but with explication of developmental changes in thought structures and the influence of these structures on performance. This emphasis suggests a variety of specific performances on which to focus instructional attention, and also suggests hypotheses concerning the optimal character and sequence of instructional attempts. In contrast, most psychometric tests of intelligence and aptitude consist of items chosen because of their predictive power rather than their relationship to observed or hypothesized intellectual processes. Thus, they offer few concrete suggestions as to what or how to teach. It appears, then, that successful attempts to adapt instruction to individual differences will depend upon a line of research emphasizing process variables in human performance.

There are other forms of evidence which contribute to our definition of the "new aptitudes" or processes for adaptive education. The fact that our concept of intelligence is undergoing significant change is obvious in the work of Piaget and in related work, but different areas of endeavor also show this clearly. There has been intensive activity in the field of comparative psychology on the intelligence of different animal species (Lockard, 1971). What used to be called general animal intelligence, and tested in the old experiments as general problem-solving ability, now appears to be an aggregate of special specific abilities, each ability evolving in response to environmental demands. Animals are "intelligent" in quite different ways that can be better understood in relation to the ecological demands of their particular environments than in terms of the older notion of a phyletic ordering of animals according to their intelligence. For example, because of their environmental demands, wasps are superior in delayed-response problems to Norway rats, and gophers are better at maze problems than horses and other open-range animals. Animals show a great many different talents evolved as adaptations to their different worlds. The older work in animal behavior appears to have overemphasized abstractions like general maze brightness as a criterion behavior for study. More recent work suggests that natural selection affects smaller mechanisms of behavior which permit the individual organism to perfect a behavior pattern adaptive to the detailed circumstances of the situation.

This fact of ecological validity, that is, that the demands of the environ-

ment influence behavior quite particularly, is apparent in another interpretation of intelligence. In a recent book on cognitive development by
Olson (1970), intelligence is defined as the elaboration of the perceptual
world that occurs in the context of acquiring skills with cultural media.
Intelligence is developed through mastering and obtaining skill in the
specifics of the prevalent media in society. Such an interpretation has been
popularized by McLuhan (1964), who points out that we tend to confuse
skill in the medium that happens to be ascendent in our own culture with
a presumed universal structure of intelligence. In this sense, intelligence
is specific to the particular ways in which school subjects can be learned.

The rise of the "new aptitudes" is also forecast by the notion of inter-
actionism whereby accommodative changes in an individual's performance
occur in the course of encounters with environmental circumstances. This
has been emphasized by such diverse points of view as Piaget's and Skinner's,
and currently is well expressed by Bandura in his writings on social learning
theory (Bandura, 1969, 1971). We know now that psychological functioning
is a continuing reciprocal interaction between the behavior of an organism
and the controlling conditions in the environment. Behavior partly creates
the environment, and the resultant environment influences the behavior.
This is clearly seen in social interaction, for example, where a person plays
an active role in bringing out a positive or negative response in others and,
in this way, creates, to some degree, environmental contingencies for himself through his own behavior. This is a two-way causal process in which
the environment might be just as influenceable as the behavior it regulates.
The actual environment an individual experiences can be a function of his
behavior if the environment is an adaptive one.

Our penchant for a fixed educational mode arises in part from an old-
fashioned psychology, from the scientific and social tendency to think in
terms of fixed categories of human beings with consistent drives and dispositions (Mischel, 1969). We think this way rather than in terms of human
beings who are highly responsive to the conditions around them so that
as conditions change or conditions are maintained, individuals act accordingly.
Adaptive educational environments can take advantage of the fact that individuals show great subtlety in adapting their competencies to different situations, if the situation permits such adaptability. Although individuals show
generalized consistent behavior on the basis of which we frequently characterize them, this does not preclude their also being very good at discriminating
and reacting to a variety of experiences in different ways. The traditional
measures of general ability and aptitudes err on the side of assuming too
much consistency, and de-emphasize the capability of individuals to devise
plans and actions depending upon the rules, needs, and demands of alternative situations. If, in our thinking about individual differences, we make as
much room for the capability of individuals to adapt and change, as well as

to be stable, and as much room for the capacity for self-regulation and self-development, as well as for victimization by enduring traits, then an adaptive notion of education must follow. An educational system should present alternative environments that enhance the ability of the individual for self-regulation in different possible situations for learning.

## ADAPTIVE EDUCATIONAL ENVIRONMENTS

So far, I have tried to show that the state of our understanding of human behavior has in some sense precluded a fruitful approach to individualization and adaptive education. For the reasons I have outlined, we have been fixed on an essentially selective mode of education and on the concepts that underlie it. I have also attempted to indicate some directions that have been taken and some milestones that we seem to have passed that appear to make change toward our ideals for adaptive education more feasible than heretofore.

While I have so far stressed fundamental research understandings, progress will not occur by research alone. The design and development of operating educational institutions is also required. Throughout history, science and technology, research and application have forced each other's hands, and mutually beneficial relationships between the two are absolutely necessary for the development of new forms of education. The development effort with which I am most familiar is the work that my colleagues and I at the University of Pittsburgh have been carrying out for some years in the design of elementary school environments that are adaptive to individual differences. This work has been described and disseminated in a variety of ways (Bolvin and Glaser, 1971; Cooley, 1971; Glaser, 1968; Lindvall and Cox, 1969; Resnick, 1967). Now is not the time to go into it further, although I should say that we have had the privilege and opportunity not only to work with schools, but also to study and evaluate our efforts so that we might move in successive approximations toward understanding what an adaptive educational environment is, how it can be designed and built, and what is the nature of the cognitive and noncognitive processes of young children that must be considered.

At the present time, certain requirements are emerging that contrast the design of an adaptive educational environment with more traditional forms of education in the elementary school. Briefly stated, some of these appear to be the following:

1. *The teaching of self-management skills and the design of educational settings in which learning-to-learn skills are fostered.* The premise here is that children can modify an environment for their own learning requirements if they command the skills to do so. For this purpose, children can be taught how to search for useful information and how to order and organize it for

learning and retention. In the selection of content for the elementary school, preference can be given to information and skills that maximize the possibilities for learning new things. The orientation and attending skills of children can be encouraged so that they learn to identify the relevant aspects of tasks and can attend to them with little distraction. With such information and skills, children can help guide the process of adaptive education.

2. *The teaching of basic psychological processes.* I have indicated this throughout my discussion. We have assumed for too long the stability of "basic aptitudes"; now we need to determine how these talents can be encouraged and taught. At the Olympic Games, young men and women joyfully exceed existing limits of human capability; in the intellectual sphere, this is also possible. The talents of individuals can be extended so that they can be provided with increased possibilities for education.

3. *The design of flexible curricula with many points of entry, different methods of instruction, and options among instructional objectives.* Extensive sequential curricula that must be used as complete systems and into which entry at different points is difficult will give way to more "modular" organizations of instructional units. This does not imply the abandonment of sequence requirements inherent in the structure of the material to be learned, but does imply that prerequisites, where essential, are to be specified in terms of capabilities of the learner rather than in terms of previous instructional experiences. A flexible curriculum avoids the necessity for all individuals to proceed through all steps in a curriculum sequence, and adapts to the fact that some individuals acquire prerequisites on their own, while others need more formal support to establish the prerequisites for more advanced learning. In such a system, it should be easy to incorporate new and varied instructional materials and objectives as they are developed in response to the changing educational interests and requirements of both teachers and students (Resnick, 1972).

4. *Increased emphasis on open testing and behaviorally indexed assessment.* In an adaptive environment, tests designed primarily to compare and select students can be expected to play a decreasing role, since access to particular educational activities will be based on a student's background together with his command of prerequisite competencies. Tests will be designed to provide information directly to the learner and the teacher to guide further learning. These tests will have an intrinsic character of openness in that they will serve as a display of the competencies to be acquired, and the results will be open to the student who can use this knowledge of his performance as a yardstick of his developing ability. These tests also will assess more than the narrow band of traditional academic outcomes. Measures of process and style, of cognitive and noncognitive development, and of performance in more

natural settings than exist in the traditional school will be required. Fortunately, this trend in process-oriented, broad-band assessment is now discernible in many new efforts.

In conclusion, it should be said that the nature of a society determines the nature of the educational system that it fosters, and educational systems tend to feed into the existing social practices. If this is so, then an adaptive educational system carried to its ultimate conclusion may be out of joint with the present social structure. An adaptive environment assumes many ways of succeeding and many goals available from which to choose. It assumes further that no particular way of succeeding is greatly valued over the other. In our current selective environment, it is quite clear that the way of succeeding that is most valued is within the relatively fixed system provided. Success in society is defined primarily in terms of the attainment of occupations directly related to the products of this system. School-related occupations are the most valued, the most rewarding, and seen as the most desirable. However, if an adaptive mode becomes prevalent and wider constellations of human abilities are emphasized, then success will have to be differently defined; many more alternative ways of succeeding will have to be appropriately rewarded than is presently the case.

Finally, basic analysis of what I have called the "new aptitudes" and the design of adaptive environments for learning is the work that is before us. The kinds of educational systems that we can consider most desirable will be drawn only from the fullest possible understanding of human behavior and from sustained, carefully studied educational innovations with the flexibility for successive incremental improvement. The traditional formulations of the nature of individual differences in learning and the traditional modes of education fail to provide enough freedom for the exercise of individual talents. We admire individual performance, but we must do more than merely stand in admiration; we must design the effective conditions under which individuals are provided with the opportunities and rewards to perform at their best and in their way.

# REFERENCES

Angoff, W. H. (Ed.). *The College Board Admissions Testing Program: A technical report on research and development activities relating to the Scholastic Aptitude Test and Achievement Tests.* New York: College Entrance Examination Board, 1971.

Bandura, A. *Principles of behavior modification.* New York: Holt, Rinehart & Winston, 1969.

———. *Social learning theory.* New York: McCaleb-Seiler, 1971.

Bolvin, J. O., and Glaser, R. Individualized instruction. In D. W. Allen and E. Seifman (Eds.), *The teacher's handbook.* Glenview, Illinois: Scott, Foresman, 1971. Pp. 270–279.

Bracht, G. H. *The relationship of treatment tasks, personological variables and dependent variables to aptitude-treatment interaction.* Boulder: University of Colorado, Laboratory of Educational Research, 1969.

———, and Glass, G. V. The external validity of experiments. *American Educational Research Journal,* 1968, 5, 437–474.

Cooley, W. W. Methods of evaluating school innovations. Invited address presented at the meeting of the American Psychological Association, Washington, D. C., September 1971.

Cronbach, L. J. The two disciplines of scientific psychology. Address of the president at the meeting of the American Psychological Association, New York, September 1957.

———. *Essentials of psychological testing.* (3rd ed.) New York: Harper & Row, 1970.

———, and Gleser, G. C. *Psychological tests and personnel decisions.* (2nd ed.) Urbana: University of Illinois Press, 1965.

———, and Snow, R. E. *Individual differences in learning ability as a function of instructional variables.* Stanford: Stanford University, School of Education, 1969.

Getzels, J. W. Pre-school education. *Teachers College Record,* 1966, 68, 219–228.

Glaser, R. Adapting the elementary school curriculum to individual performance. In *Proceedings of the 1967 Invitational Conference on Testing Problems.* Princeton: Educational Testing Service, 1968. Pp. 3–36.

———, and Resnick, L. B. Instructional psychology. In P. H. Mussen and M. R. Rosenzweig (Eds.), *Annual review of psychology.* Palo Alto: Annual Reviews, 1972. Pp. 207–276.

Kagan, J., and Kogan, N. Individual variation in cognitive processes. In P. H. Mussen (Ed.), *Carmichael's manual of child psychology,* Volume 1. (3rd ed.) New York: John Wiley, 1970. Pp. 1273–1365.

Lindvall, C. M., and Cox, R. C. The role of evaluation in programs for individualized instruction. In *Sixty-eighth Yearbook of the National Society for the Study of Education, Part II.* Chicago: NSSE, 1969. Pp. 156–188.

Lockard, R. B. Reflections on the fall of comparative psychology: Is there a message for us all? *American Psychologist,* 1971, 26, 168–179.

McLuhan, M. *Understanding media: The extensions of man.* Toronto: McGraw-Hill, 1964.

McNemar, Q. Lost: Our intelligence? Why? *American Psychologist,* 1964, 19, 871–882.

Meichenbaum, D. H. *The nature and modification of impulsive children: Training impulsive children to talk to themselves.* Ontario: Univerity of Waterloo, Department of Psychology, 1971.

————, and Goodman, J. Reflection-impulsivity and verbal control of motor behavior. *Child Development,* 1969, *40,* 785–797.

Melton, A. W. Individual differences and theoretical process variables: General comments on the conference. In R. M. Gagné (Ed.), *Learning and individual differences.* Columbus: Charles E. Merrill, 1967. Pp. 238–252.

Mischel, W. Continuity and change in personality. *American Psychologist,* 1969, *24,* 1012–1018.

Olson, D. R. *Cognitive development: The child's acquisition of diagonality.* New York: Academic Press, 1970.

Resnick, L. B. *Design of an early learning curriculum.* Pittsburgh: University of Pittsburgh, Learning Research and Development Center, 1967.

————. Open education: Some tasks for technology. *Educational Technology,* 1972, *12* (1), 70–76.

Rohwer, W. D., Jr. Images and pictures in children's learning. *Psychological Bulletin,* 1970, 73, 393–403. (a)

————. Mental elaboration and proficient learning. In J. P. Hill (Ed.), *Minnesota symposia on child psychology.* Minneapolis: University of Minnesota, 1970. Pp. 220–260. (b)

————. Learning, race and school success. *Review of Educational Research,* 1971, *41,* 191–210.

Rosner, J. *A formative evaluation of the Perceptual Skills Curriculum Project.* Pittsburgh: University of Pittsburgh, Learning Research and Development Center, 1972.

Thorndike, E. L. *Individuality.* Boston: Houghton Mifflin, 1911.

Tyler, L. E. *The psychology of human differences.* (3rd ed.) New York: Appleton-Century-Crofts, 1965.

Washburne, C. N. Adapting the schools to individual differences. In *Twenty-fourth Yearbook of the National Society for the Study of Education, Part II.* Chicago: NSSE, 1925.

Wing, C. W., Jr., and Wallach, M. A. *College admissions and the psychology of talent.* New York: Holt, Rinehart & Winston, 1971.

Yando, R. M., and Kagan, J. The effect of teacher tempo on the child. *Child Development,* 1968, *39,* 27–34.

# III

## ALTERNATIVE DIRECTIONS FOR RESEARCH IN INSTRUCTION AND TEACHING

# 5

# Children and Adolescents: Should We Teach Them or Let Them Learn?

## WILLIAM D. ROHWER, JR.

We are largely ignorant when it comes to answering questions about vital issues in education. What should be taught? When should it be taught? How should it be taught? To whom should it be taught? What are the consequences of teaching this rather than that, of teaching it now rather than then, of teaching it this way rather than that way, to this person as well as to that person? If candid, our professional response to these questions is that we don't know. Indeed, we might even take some measure of pride in this response. As researchers, it is fitting to disclaim possession of final answers and to advertise the boundaries of our knowledge. Thus, we can justly enjoy good feelings about declaring the modesty of our wisdom. But whatever comfort we derive from this honest statement of our limitations, it cannot last long because we are also committed to making significant reductions in our ignorance.

If you find this appraisal too extreme to deserve consideration, imagine yourself in the role of a trusted and respected consultant, endowed with all of the most powerful theory, evidence, information, and skills that we share collectively. Suppose a client comes to you with the questions just mentioned for the purpose of implementing your answers by establishing an entirely new system of schooling. Assume the client has all of the resources necessary for accomplishing this purpose excepting only the information he seeks from you. To inject a note of realism, let him impose two conditions: that the system should serve a population having a composition comparable to that

Excerpts from this address, originally written for the AERA, have also appeared in *The Educational Researcher* 1, no. 7 (July, 1972), 5–11.

103

in the United States; and that the maximum time he can allow you to answer the questions is ten years. Also suppose the client offers to fund your efforts to obtain answers, on whatever scale necessary, for the ten-year period. In advance, he requires only two things of you: that you explain the methods you propose to use, showing their potential for answering the questions; and that you give him your personal assurance that the probability of your success is reasonably high. Suppose that success simply means obtaining enough answers to yield some concrete proposals for a program of schooling.

Could you comply? I am not confident that I could. And the reasons for my pessimism do not seem trivial—they do not concern shortages of trained personnel, nor an inability to estimate costs, nor a fear that an interval of ten years is too short, even though it probably is. The reason is that I note precious little evidence that questions of the kind asked by the client are the questions typically addressed by educational research.

If this appraisal is accurate, it is dismaying because it seems to me that the questions posed by this client are important questions. They are obviously the same questions that are being asked currently about schooling in the United States. The imaginary client, after all, is not a product of pure fantasy. He could easily be a district superintendent, a school board chairman, or, more likely, a visible representative of the public—a community leader or a legislator. In fact, educational researchers are also fascinated by the issues the questions raise. Thus, it is tempting to wonder why the prospects for obtaining answers are not brighter.

## THE PROBLEM OF CONDUCTING DECISIVE RESEARCH

I will mention only two of the many possible reasons for the fact that research to date has produced too few answers for vital educational questions. One reason is that it may be practically impossible to do decisive research in education. Another reason is that educational researchers may be too conventional or conservative to engage in it. The first reason is especially important to those who wish to conduct research that is experimental in character. Questions about when, how, and to whom topics should be taught seem to demand the manipulation of different schooling programs so that their effects can be compared. At least the questions require that variations in schooling programs and procedures be available in nature even if they cannot be manipulated. The argument is that decisive research entails experimentation with a system, education, that is as fixed as the solar system, and therefore open only to the methods of observational science.

A fair retort to this argument is that it ignores available facts. After all, many aspects of education have been subjected to experimental analysis. Examples abound, but the subjects of reading and mathematics are good ones.

Numerous studies have manipulated instructional methods for assisting children to acquire reading skills and the results give comparatively persuasive answers about the relative merits of the methods. The advent of the "new math" has spurred many experimental contrasts of methods for teaching mathematics and such research has provided some answers. As in any field, research in the areas of reading and mathematics is of uneven quality but the solid studies have been relatively conclusive. So, what is the insurmountable practical problem alluded to?

The problem is that virtually every instance of an experimental attack on an educational issue starts by accepting conventional assumptions about schooling. How many studies are there that have addressed the question whether formal reading instruction is more effective if it begins at age ten than at age six? What would result if mathematics instruction were scheduled only during alternate years, beginning in the second grade? How would an elementary school program designed to improve interpersonal skills affect the acquisition of traditional academic skills? Do children derive more profit per year of formal instruction when they are five or when they are thirteen? Questions like these make the practical obstacles visible because the experiments they entail would disturb the ordering of current educational priorities.

Questions very similar to these have spawned experimental research but only when they could be answered without challenging the present criteria of schooling. We are now rich with data about the effects of a variety of types of early childhood education. Academic, cognitive, traditional, one-year, and two-year preschool programs have been compared with control groups and with one another. We even have some evidence about the comparative effects of different programs for different populations of children. But note two features of the studies that have provided us with this kind of evidence. One is that they all involve adding years and programs to the present structure of schooling, not deleting any from it or displacing any within it. A second feature is that the success of the various programs is mainly judged by their effects on the usual criteria of schooling—do the children read better by the end of first grade, or do they score better on IQ tests by virtue of participation in the preschool program. Thus, we are free to manipulate by experimenting with pre-first-grade programs, and probably even with post-twelfth-grade programs. But the intervening years remain largely inviolate. This is the practical obstacle.

The reality of this barrier must be admitted. Nevertheless, it need not intimidate us. It serves a useful function: to moderate runaway, and often unjustified, revisionism. Shortly, I will suggest that the barrier simply requires us to demonstrate, convincingly, that major variations in the structure of established schooling promise to improve its outcomes. If we cannot do this, we are on extremely shaky ethical grounds anyway and deserve our bonds.

This discussion of the practical constraints on progress in educational research has already touched on a second obstacle to decisive research—our own conservatism. Before trying to construct a brief for this part of the case, let me moderate my conclusion in advance. The conclusion will be that our research bears the mark of deference to conventional beliefs, and commitment to the preservation of customary practices. The qualification is that there are at least three major functions for educational research and the conclusion applies to only one of these.

The educational research community is already performing rather well in improving instructional methods and programs for attaining currently prescribed objectives of schooling. Evidence that this function is being fulfilled and that additional progress should be anticipated can be found in a number of examples (see, for example, Beck and Mitroff, 1972; Resnick, Wang, and Kaplan, 1970; Weikart, 1971). These examples are noteworthy for the degree of success achieved, the conception that has guided them, and for the fact that they have been attentive to the needs of students who vary widely in background characteristics such as developmental rate, socioeconomic status (SES), and ethnicity.

Another research function is also represented visibly in the work of our community. Drawing on the discipline of differential psychology, many of our members persistently pursue the sources of individual differences in educational outcomes. At present, for example, we are witness to a fairly lively set of controversies that have centered on a publication in the *Harvard Educational Review* by Arthur Jensen (1969). Judging by the number and variety of persons who have gotten into this act, we are deeply involved in the task of accounting for variation in school success when the criteria are the customary ones of performance on IQ and school achievement tests.

Unfortunately, a third potential function of educational research is not adequately realized. This function may be described as that of fostering change in the basic framework of schooling. It seems proper for the research community to question present assumptions, propose alternative ones, provide a theoretical and empirical rationale for the alternatives, demonstrate the promise of those assumptions, and evaluate the consequences of implementing the assumptions. Bluntly, we ought to engage in a sustained and effective challenge to the status quo. Proposals for radical change in schooling may be plentiful enough to be regarded as constituting a movement, but, if so, the educational research community is not in the vanguard.

Let me try to be clear on this point. I am not suggesting that we are obliged to excel at the kind of rhetoric and the kind of radicalism that pervades the semi-popular educational literature. Instead, I am proposing that a proper function for the educational research community is to debate the vital issues of education, free of the constraints of present assumptions. Moreover, such discussion should be sustained over long periods so that it can result in research designed to answer the questions raised by the issues.

As I see it, the main obstacle to progress in this regard is that too many of us, either tacitly or explicitly, accept the validity of present systems of schooling. We capitulate in the use of end-of-first-grade reading tests to evaluate the effectiveness of early childhood programs. When disproportionate numbers of children from poor homes fail in school, we may complain that instruction is inadequate, but what we do, at least visibly, is to ascribe the failure to the child's disadvantage. We recommend that he enter school earlier to compensate for the disadvantage. Or we control for his disadvantage by showing that he succeeds as well as can be expected given his low IQ. Either way, the present criteria and procedures of instruction remain unscathed.

Perhaps we hesitate to challenge the validity of the current frameworks of schooling because of the weight of supporting evidence. Perhaps, but probably not. We know as well or better than others that most of the evidence is far from compelling. Elsewhere (Rohwer, 1971) I have argued that one of the chief kinds of evidence, the relationship between educational attainment and occupational placement, may be freely regarded with great skepticism. To be sure, the relationship is a strong one but it may be artifactual. The reason is that educational attainment determines the level of entry into occupational hierarchies. Within such levels, the relationship between school performance and occupational proficiency is marginal at best. Most other ways of demonstrating the validity of schooling are equally suspect. The relationship between school performance and IQ, for example, is patently circular. Thus, the evidence is not sufficient to inhibit us. We are free to question existing frameworks and proceed from there.

Such questioning is already evident in recent statements of some educational researchers. Although I disagree with his formulation, one instance is provided by Jensen's (1969, 1971) conclusion that a major alternative form of instruction must be developed. Another example may be found in Bereiter's (1969) proposal that education be abolished in favor of teaching only those skills that can, in fact, be taught successfully to virtually all children. Glaser (1972) has presented a persuasive brief for displacing the selective model that currently controls the structure of schooling with an adaptive model. Encouraging instances like these are no longer hard to come by. But, until we can sustain the discussion, a coherent body of radical theory and research will not emerge. So far, we have not done so.

At present, too little of our research is decisive for questions of what should be taught, when it should be taught, and for estimating the consequences of answering the questions one way rather than another. For example, consider Humphreys' (1971) recent assertions that, ". . . Subject-matter knowledge or skills in these areas [arithmetic, history, science] is not a necessary, perhaps not even a useful, goal for the first six grades. . . . Formal teaching, or learning of arithmetic can be delayed until the seventh grade, and all of the learning required for starting high school mathematics can be accomplished by the end of the eighth grade. . . . By the end of the sixth grade it is better that a child like science than that he know a great deal about science." There are three or four different assertions in this single quotation, every one important in the sense that it implies a drastic change in schooling. But I am unable to find any data that can be used to verify the assertions, one way or the other.

To take another example, entertain the hypothesis that children would become more skillful readers if reading instruction began at age nine or ten rather than at five or six. At present we have no data that are directly relevant to the hypothesis; the necessary research has not been done. We are beginning to obtain evidence about the effects of starting reading instruction earlier than usual but there is no indication on the horizon that we will ever learn about the consequences of starting it later than usual. We know that the earlier in school a child becomes an accomplished reader, the better his chances for succeeding in the other school subjects. For all we know, however, this may be due entirely to the fact that instruction in other subjects relies so heavily on printed educational materials.

Another variation on this theme emerges in our tactics for dealing with individual differences. If there is reason to suspect that a child will encounter substantial difficulty in learning to read, we prescribe a larger dose of instruction, at an earlier age, than for a child who is likely to learn with ease. The rationale for writing this prescription, however, is no more compelling than for another one—that the child should receive reading instruction at a later age. How are we to choose between these two prescriptions? Properly designed research studies could provide a basis for choice, but they have not been conducted. On an issue like this one, that is, the optimal timing for instruction, our research does not appear to be relevant. If this is true, it is a clear and present obstacle to progress.

It is easy to conceive of research that would be decisive for vital questions about education. Genius is not required to design studies that would resolve issues such as the proper timing of instruction or tailoring instructional timing to individual differences. The problem is that such studies appear to risk the survival of the children who might participate in them. Parents, educators, legislators accurately perceive that failure in school drastically limits the range of choices available to those who fail. Thus, they would be right to oppose many conceivable experimental studies of education. Imagine a study, for example, that included a comparison of different ages for the onset of reading instruction, say age ten versus age six, for a representative sample of children from rich homes and another of children from poor homes. The consternation this proposal would arouse in concerned parties would be perfectly understandable.

Dozens of other examples of decisive research studies could easily be constructed. But the exercise is pointless unless there is some means of gaining the cooperation necessary to conduct the studies. If we wish to conduct decisive research we have no choice but to deal with the practical obstacles that bar the way.

## AN AVENUE TO DECISIVE RESEARCH

Consider two research objectives: (a) determining the optimal time for beginning formal instruction about some skill or topic, and (b) determining how this schedule should be varied in order to adapt to individual differences. To accomplish these objectives in terms that bear directly on specific school subjects such as reading and arithmetic, research studies must eventually include tasks drawn from those subjects. Because of practical obstacles, however, we cannot begin with such studies. We must first find ways of providing assurance that children who participate in them stand to benefit more than they stand to lose. And to give assurance, we need to have some verifiable convictions about the development of mental processes in children and about the role of instruction in activating those processes. I should like to address this matter by means of a case study that illustrates one strategy for gaining verifiable convictions. This strategy involves engaging in a program of empirical research in cognitive development and in a systematic reexamination of the available research literature in that domain.

The research program to be described is characterized by five features considered to be critical for opening a path to the resolution of fundamental educational issues. These critical features may be summarized as follows:

1. *Cumulative Research.* The program of research should be planned so that the same kind of task may be used repeatedly. The reason for this is that it serves an intent to specify the underlying process responsible for observable performances. If a variety of tasks are to be used, there should be at a minimum, clear reason to believe that the same process is being tapped from task to task.

2. *Developmental Research.* Given the first feature, studies should examine task performance across as wide a developmental range as possible. The purpose, of course, is to detect performance changes that might signal important developmental shifts in underlying processes.

3. *Experimental Research.* Because the ultimate aim of the program

concerns instruction, we need to know the effects of various experimental conditions on performance. In particular, we need to know the identity of conditions that produce optimal performance on the tasks used or that optimally activate the processes responsible for that performance.

4. *Comparative Research.*   Assuming that the research program is cumulative, developmental, and experimental, it should also be comparative because we want to make inferences about individual differences. That is, we need information about the range of variation across different kinds of children that is associated with the effects of different experimental conditions at different ages.

5. *Realistic Research.*   Finally, the proposed strategy is based on a key assumption: the optimal timing of formal instruction will be indicated by evidence that the underlying process necessary for successful task performance is available in a substantial proportion of the population. In other words, we are not seeking ways of making children precocious but ways of assisting them to be optimally effective.

The case illustration is a research program concerned with the development of learning processes in children and adolescents. It will be described in terms of several steps to highlight the principal components of the proposed strategy for developing a means to conduct decisive research. To be presented first is a description of the task most often used in the research program. Then the assumptions that launched the program will be enumerated and contrasted with the conclusions that have resulted from it. Next, an account will be given of the effort made to specify the underlying process responsible for task performance. The process description will then be used to characterize developmental and individual differences in task performance. Finally, a process of deriving instructional hypotheses will be illustrated. The essence of the proposed strategy is that basic research can be used to generate instructional hypotheses that are believable enough to gain public support for decisive research, research involving direct experimentation with instruction.

## The Task

The task typically used in the illustrative research program involves presenting to the student a list of paired words, such as *bat-cup* and *arrow-glasses*, directing him to study the pairs, then testing him by presenting one word from each pair and asking that he supply the missing words. Such paired-associate tasks are often used in laboratory research on human verbal learning and memory. In recent years, they have also appeared in a number of studies designed to analyze the development of learning processes in children. Even though they are ostensibly simple, paired-associate tasks appear to involve processes that are common to other, more complicated tasks. For example, significant correlations have been observed between paired-associate performance and reading achievement in the early primary grades (Lambert, 1970; Rohwer and Levin, 1971) as well as with IQ test performance at several age levels: kindergarten through grade three (Rohwer, Ammon, Suzuki and Levin, 1971); grade six (Rohwer, 1966); and grade twelve. Moreover, when college students are interviewed after learning a list of paired-associates, they report using a variety of strategies to master the task. These two lines of evidence imply that the task of paired-associates taps processes that are conceptual in character and that are relevant to schooling. On the other hand, students do not commonly receive direct instruction in how to learn associations between unrelated pairs of words. Thus the task is a handy one for the purpose of analyzing the development of learning processes and for determining the effects of instruction on performance. It draws on processes implicated in at least some school subject learning, but it is relatively free of the effects of within-school instruction.

### Original Assumptions and Recent Conclusions

The early stages of our work were guided by several assumptions (cf., Rohwer, 1967, 1968). It is instructive to state these in order to make clear the manner in which they were forcibly altered by the kind of inquiry proposed. Three of the assumptions are of particular interest.

a. Several different underlying processes are responsible for performance on the task. These processes vary in terms of modality—verbal versus imagery —and in complexity—rote versus conceptual. Thus, efficient performance was thought to result from one kind of process and inefficient performance from another.

b. Developmentally, the shift from inefficient processes to efficient ones was presumed to occur commonly over the age range four to seven years.

c. In this age range, individual differences in other kinds of learning, learning to read, for example, were assumed to be related to individual differences in the efficiency of the process whereby children learn paired associates. Thus, it was predicted that low-SES students would perform more poorly than high-SES students on paired-associate tasks. Furthermore, it was expected that special instruction in techniques for learning, especially if given during this early age range, would assist low-SES children to perform as well as high-SES children.

At present, no one of these assumptions seems tenable (Rohwer, in press). Instead, the facts call for substituting three very different assumptions.

a.   A single underlying process, which I call *elaboration,* is responsible when paired associates are learned. Therefore, the efficiency of performance is determined by whether or not the elaboration process is triggered.

b.   Developmental changes in paired-associate performance are not caused by changes in the character of the underlying process. Rather, they reflect changes in the conditions required to trigger the single process. The process itself is available from at least age four on. But there are three important developmental shifts in the kinds of conditions required to activate elaboration. Only one of these typically occurs in the age range four to seven years; another averages between seven and nine; and the other appears much later, usually between twelve and sixteen years.

c.   There are individual differences in the conditions required to activate elaboration. But, during childhood, that is, from approximately four to twelve years, these differences relate little, if at all, to classifications like SES or ethnicity. The average age of the developmental shift during childhood appears relatively constant across a number of different populations. In contrast, the later developmental shift does appear to be related to SES, it appears to emerge earlier for high-SES than for low-SES students. Even so, it can be demonstrated convincingly that the process of elaboration is available in virtually everyone, regardless of group membership or within-group individual differences.

Let me try to indicate what forced the change in assumptions and draw out some implications of the changes. Before doing so, however, it is important to mention one feature of our approach that has not changed over the last ten years. That is, a prominent research objective has been to discover conditions that produce optimal performance on the task. In this sense, the approach is directly oriented to instructional considerations, that is, to the question how best to assist students in achieving mastery.

### Specifying an Underlying Process

Given the production of optimal performance as a criterion, the original first assumption was readily discredited. Studies began to show that optimal performance on a paired-associate task could be achieved by virtually all subjects, regardless of age or background, depending only on the implementation of the proper task conditions. In one study, for example (Irwin, 1971) the use of peculiarly effective learning conditions produced optimal performance in five-year-olds that was equivalent to that observed in eleven-year-olds. (And the outcome was not produced by an artificial ceiling effect.) It is worth mentioning the conditions necessary for this result. All children were asked to learn a list of 32 noun pairs. The nouns were not just presented as words, however; each one was represented by an object it denoted. Furthermore, as the experimenter displayed a pair of objects, he enacted an episode involving them. In the case of *bat-cup*, for example, he placed the handle end of the bat in the cup. After one presentation of the pairs in this manner, the five-year-olds, as well as the eleven-year-olds, scored approximately 81 percent correct responses on the average, an impressive level of performance indeed (cf., Wolff and Levin, in press).

In order to specify an underlying process, however, it is not enough to know the conditions sufficient for optimal task performance. It is also important to identify conditions in which optimal performance does not occur. This has been done using the task just described: the learning of noun pairs. If the pairs are represented only by orally presented words and if the only assistance provided by the experimenter is the instruction to learn the pairs, the average performance of groups of five-year-olds will be very poor. After a single presentation of the list, less than 10 percent of their responses will be correct. In fact, when the task is presented this way, available research suggests that optimal performance is achieved only by students who obtain high scores on IQ tests and even then not until these students are between fourteen and seventeen years of age. Thus, the two versions of this single task yield results that are markedly discrepant.

The question of interest is how to account for the discrepancy. One way is to assume that different processes are at work in the two versions of the task. A related assumption would be that one of these processes is available to all persons, including five-year-olds, while the other is available only to high-IQ persons beyond the age of sixteen. Some may wish to maintain such a hypothesis but I find it uncongenial for two reasons. First, it seems needlessly complicated. More important, however, it seems unreasonable to believe that two distinctly different processes are involved when (a) the task itself remains the same (coupling together unrelated pairs of nouns) and (b) optimal performance can be produced simply by arranging the proper conditions for learning. Thus, I much prefer the hypothesis that performance on the task is determined by whether or not the one necessary underlying process is activated, rather than by which of several different underlying processes is activated.

Suppose we adopt the position that a single conceptual process is responsible for the production of correct responses on noun-pair tasks. It still remains to find a way of explaining the discrepant results obtained with different versions of the task, and also of explaining the discrepant results observed across different individuals. To accomplish this, it is probably useful to construct a more detailed description of the character of the hypothesized underlying process. Start with the end product of the process, namely, the coupling together of pairs of items that were initially unrelated. Assume that this coupling is achieved by generating an event that integrally involves both of the items. Call this process *elaboration*. That is, the elaboration process consists of generating an event that serves as a common referent for the items to be coupled. The term event refers to an episode that integrates one or more objects or actors into a common relationship. When this process is activated for any pair of items, the items will be learned, when it is not activated, the pair will not be learned. The key for explaining discrepant results across versions of the task and across varieties of individuals then, lies in the triggering conditions necessary to activate the process of elaboration.

A review of the research literature in this area suggests that triggering conditions can be ordered in terms of how explicitly they prompt the subject to generate referential events for the items to be learned. From study to study, task conditions vary with respect to how explicitly they prompt elaboration, and persons vary in how explicit the prompt must be to elicit elaboration.

Further analysis suggests that we can account for most of the reported phenomena by distinguishing four degrees of prompt explicitness: maximal, substantial, moderate, and minimal. At the maximal level, the task conditions include an actual demonstration of an event to be generated for each pair of items to be coupled. A substantial prompt involves presenting a description or representation, either by means of words or pictures, of an event for each pair. A moderate prompt consists of directing the subject to think of an event that integrates the pairs of items. And a minimal prompt simply instructs the subject to learn and remember the pairs.

### The Elaboration Process, Developmental Trends, and Individual Differences

It is now possible to see how this analysis can be used to describe developmental and individual differences in performance on noun-pair tasks. The displays in Figure 1 are useful for this purpose. The picture presented there is an idealization of actual data, but on the whole it only smooths out reality rather than violating it. The columns at each age level represent groups of students from high-SES backgrounds (upper panel) as well as groups of students from low-SES backgrounds (lower panel). Note that at every age level for both these populations at least one of the columns reaches the hypothetical level designated as "Optimal Performance." The different kinds of shading within the columns indicate the explicitness of the prompts required to produce that level of performance. At the earliest age, for example, maximal prompts, the solid columns, are essential for optimal performance. By about age 7, the criterion can nearly be met with substantially explicit prompts, represented by striped columns. By age 9, continuing through age 12, moderately explicit prompts (stippled columns) are almost sufficient. Note

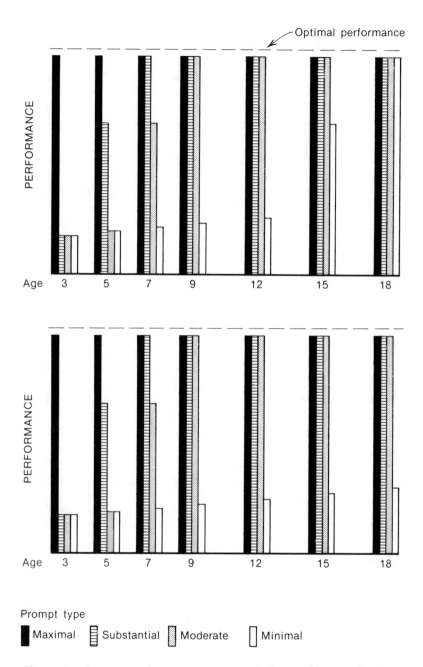

*Figure 1.* Summary of prompt types required to achieve optimal performance as a function of age. Schematic patterns for high-SES (upper panel) and low-SES (lower panel) populations.

too that through age 12, the picture for low-SES students is identical in all essential respects with that for high-SES students. Thus, there is no evidence here to support the claim that the two populations differ, in the childhood age range, either in the kind of underlying process responsible for optimal performance or in the reactivity of the process to various kinds of prompts.

It can be seen that the relative effectiveness of maximal, substantial, and moderate prompts remains fairly constant across the range from 12 to 18 years. For high-SES students, the marked shift during this period is in minimal prompts. By the end of the period, minimal prompts are sufficient for optimal performance whereas at the beginning of the period, at least moderately explicit prompts are required. The general trend across the entire range, from early childhood to adulthood, is characterized by marked increases in the extent to which the elaboration process is self-activating. At the beginning, there is virtually complete dependence on maximally explicit prompts; by the end, there is almost complete autonomy from explicit prompts.

In the adolescent age range, a substantial between-groups difference is evident in the effectiveness of minimal prompts. The shift for the high-SES group contrasts sharply with the continuing insufficiency of minimal prompts for the low-SES group, even after age 12. This difference in the average developmental pattern for the two populations appears to be quite reliable. The interpretation of the difference, however, is disputable. I regard as insupportable the claim that differences in underlying capability are responsible for the discrepant effectiveness of minimal prompts for the two populations, since it is too difficult to square this interpretation with the fact that only a moderate prompt—the suggestion to the subject that he generate an event— is necessary to produce optimal performance. The equivalent effectiveness of such moderate prompts seems to me to demonstrate that the underlying capability is distributed equally in both populations. Thus, rather than stemming from a difference in underlying process, the source of the phenomenon appears to be that members of one group have acquired a propensity for autonomous activation of the elaboration process while members of the other group have not learned this skill.

The facts here are reminiscent of those produced by research using tasks that presumably tap formal operations in the Piagetian sense. Analogous differences among populations led Goodnow (1971) to conclude that the discrepancies are explainable in terms of whether or not "tricks of the trade" have been learned for dealing with the problems presented by the tasks. Similarly, the interpretation I am suggesting for the results of research on noun-pair learning asserts that many persons do not learn the trick of triggering the elaboration process whenever they are confronted by tasks demanding that they couple together disparate items of information.

*Deriving Instructional Hypotheses*

It is obviously premature to base definite instructional recommendations on the results and interpretation of a single research program. Nevertheless, this case study can be used to illustrate the process of deriving instructional hypotheses from basic research. Let me reiterate that the goal of the proposed strategy is not to establish a direct link from basic research to educational change. Instead, it is to use basic research to demonstrate the promise of particular changes so that decisive research can be done to directly evaluate their effects.

In thinking about the implications of research on noun-pair learning, it will be helpful to look again at the summary provided in Figure 1. One of the prominent implications suggested by this display is that a distinction be made between two kinds of learning: the learning of specific content on the one hand and the learning of skills useful for acquiring specific content on the other. With regard to the learning of specific content, the implications of the research seem unequivocal. If the content is important enough that we require children to learn it, we are obliged to design instruction that will make learning optimal. For some children, younger children for example, instructional prompts must be more explicit than for other children. But, according to the information in the figure, we can discharge the obligation for virtually all children, regardless of age or background. That is, for both populations, at every age level shown, some of the columns invariably reach the level of optimal performance; in every case, the students have mastered the content with ease and efficiency.

Consider an example pertinent to this point about content learning. Recently Robert Matz and I conducted an experiment that tests the generality of the elaboration interpretation of noun-pair learning. In this study, the task was to listen to three short passages of expository prose and to answer eight true-false questions about each passage. We viewed the task as requiring the listener to generate events as common referents for the information in the passages, that is, we assumed that an elaboration process was involved in performing the task. Accordingly, we manipulated the kind of prompt presented along with the oral rendition of the passages that was given to all the children. In one condition, the printed text of the passage was presented as it was read aloud to the child. In the other condition, the information in each passage was represented pictorially as the prose was read aloud to the child. Since we believe that the elaboration process is more easily triggered in many children by pictorial rather than printed prompts, we predicted that performance would be better in the pictorial condition. Note, however, that with regard to content learning, the task was identical in both prompt conditions, namely, to comprehend and remember the information in the passage.

We sampled subjects from two populations of fourth-grade children: one from a school serving a high-SES white community, and the other from a school serving a low-SES black community. We knew in advance that the two groups differed by about two grade levels in terms of performance on standardized tests of reading achievement. So, we took the precaution of including in the passages only words that could be accurately identified in their printed form by children from both populations.

The results corroborated our predictions. In the printed text condition, the high-SES white sample produced an average of 82 percent correct responses; in the pictorial condition, the average was 90 percent. The difference between the two prompt conditions was even more dramatic for the low-SES black children: the text prompt produced only 58 percent correct responses—a very low level of performance considering the fact that chance level on the true-false test was 50 percent correct. In the pictorial condition, however, a near-optimal level of performance was achieved: an average of 81 percent correct responses.

Thus, on this task of comprehending prose passages, mastery of the specific content was assured, for both samples, by establishing effective prompt conditions. Had this been a real task, that is, one required of the child in school, the instructional obligation would be to present the content so that it could be learned easily and efficiently. This much is clear. For if the content were critical for subsequent learning, say for participating in an exercise in science observation, improper presentation would effectively deny many children the opportunity to profit from the next experience.

Besides illustrating implications for content learning, the outcome of this study also emphasizes the importance of skill learning. Especially in the sample of low-SES black children, the skill of activating elaboration given a printed text prompt—in other words, the skill of reading—had not been successfully acquired. Does basic research in cognitive development have implications for instruction in the acquisition of skills?

Looking at Figure 1 again, it appears the answer is "Yes." Keep in mind that in the elaboration model a skill consists of a high degree of sensitivity to prompts of low degrees of explicitness. The "skill" that increases across the age range shown is a series of progressive decreases in the threshold for triggering the elaboration process. The research suggests that this skill is a reasonable one to acquire: virtually all people appear to acquire it to a considerable degree and many people appear to acquire it completely. Furthermore, it is of considerable assistance on this kind of memory task, a task that is relatively common even for adults. So the questions are: When should formal instruction in the skill be offered? and What should be the aim of instruction when it is offered?

My suggestion is that the answers to these questions about skill learning should be similar to the conclusions offered about content learning. The aim of instruction in skills should be optimal performance, that is, mastery of the skill. The timing of instruction should be chosen so as to ensure that virtually all children can attain mastery with relative ease and efficiency. This second stricture requires a modification of the first: even though the ultimate aim of skill instruction may be complete mastery of the skill, at any given age the immediate aim may be far short of mastery at a fully mature level. So, for example, the appropriate aim of instruction in elaboration skills at age seven would be to assist the child in gaining sensitivity to moderate prompts, not to free him of the need for explicit prompts of any kind.

With regard to skill instruction, my contention is that the results of experimental-developmental research offer guidance both as to the timing of instruction, the immediate aims of instruction, and the ultimate aims of instruction. The question of ultimate aims can be disposed of most easily. The ultimate aims of skill instruction should be to assist students in mastering those useful skills that substantial numbers of the adult population eventually achieve. In the case of the elaboration process, it appears that a substantial portion of the population acquires the skill of optimal performance in the presence of only minimally explicit prompts.

### A Rule of Thumb for the Timing of Instruction

Starting with that ultimate aim, the strategy is to work backwards. Thus, the next question is: When should formal instruction designed to foster this aim begin? Let me propose a rule of thumb—instruction should begin (a) only after the immediately prior skill has been mastered, and (b) when the developmental curve for the skill shows signs of rising. In other words, formal instruction should be offered to children when they are in a transition period with respect to the particular skill we wish to foster. This rule can be explicated with reference to the charts in Figure 2. The schematic curves in each panel represent increases with age in sensitivity of the elaboration process to the four type of prompts. An inspection of the figure indicates that the optimal time for introducing instruction in the skill of using minimal prompts is bracketed by the age range of 12 to 15 years. In this range students have mastered the skill of using moderate prompts to achieve optimal performance on noun-pair tasks. It is also clear that by the middle of the range, the developmental curve for a substantial number of students (upper panel) shows a sharp deflection relative to the previous age range. This deflection is the cue for introducing instruction, both for high-SES and for low-SES students.

Working backwards again, the skill immediately preceding the ultimate one is that of deriving full advantage from moderate prompts. Using the

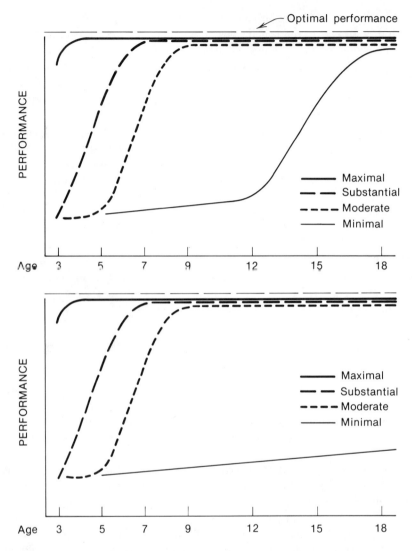

*Figure 2.   Hypothetical course of developmental changes in sensitivity to four kinds of elaborative prompts: upper panel—high-SES populations; lower panel—low-SES populations.*

proposed rule of thumb, it appears that instruction in this skill should begin at approximately age 7. Extrapolating from the figure, it can be guessed that by then, many children have fully mastered the skill of using substantial prompts, and that the curve for moderate prompts has begun to rise. Similarly, an application of the rule with respect to the use of substantial prompts suggests that instruction begin at about age 6.

Some of our research illustrates the consequences of ignoring this rule of thumb. In one study (Rohwer and Ammon, 1971) we offered formal instruction to seven-year-olds in the skill of performing optimally in the presence of minimal prompts. Although we detected statistically significant effects of instruction, the results were disappointing: the children did not come close to attaining optimal performance levels. Later, we compounded our error by offering a similar kind of instruction to four- and five-year-olds (Rohwer, Ammon and Levin, 1971). Although we improved the instructional materials and procedures over those used in the initial study, the aim was still the same—to equip the children to perform optimally given prompts that were only minimally explicit. The results showed that the two weeks of instruction were of no effect whatever. With hindsight—it is an understatement to say that our timing was bad—we should have been working with 13- or 14-year-olds. Thus, the proposed rule of thumb about the timing and aims of instruction is not without evidential support.

Consider how the proposed rule of thumb can be applied to derive hypotheses about the timing and aims of instruction in school-subject skills. Use of the rule depends on knowing five things: (a) the conditions necessary for optimal performance on the task of interest; (b) the character of the underlying process responsible for performance on the task; (c) the extent to which a substantial majority of adults possess the skill of activating the process; (d) the major landmarks along the way to achieving the final form of the skill; and (e) knowing the form of the developmental function so as to identify the ages at which the achievement of each landmark can be accomplished with ease and efficiency. At present, however, these prerequisites to successful application of the rule are not available for school subjects.

A strategy for gaining the information prerequisite to decisive research has been illustrated in terms of the case study. The strategy could be further improved by analyzing school-subject tasks to reveal their essential psychological components, creating non-school tasks that are isomorphic with these components, and conducting coherent programs of research using the new tasks. The reason for insisting on non-school tasks, of course, is that school-subject tasks cannot be used in such research until the present lock on the timing of their introduction is opened. And that lock can not be opened until we know enough to make a key.

In conclusion, I want to emphasize my agreement with Bereiter's dictum: schools should teach only what is teachable (Bereiter, 1969). But, the only way to find out what is teachable is by discovering how and when it can be learned with ease. Some may disagree with these dicta, believing that learning is not learning unless it hurts. But, I know of no evidence, and can draw on no experience, to contradict the conviction that failing to learn mainly teaches us to hate learning and, in the process, how to fail.

# REFERENCES

Beck, I., and Mitroff, D. The rationale and design of a primary grades reading system for an individualized classroom. Monograph on the Reading Project of the Learning Research and Development Center, University of Pittsburgh, 1972, in press.

Bereiter, C. A proposal to abolish education. In B. Crittenden (Ed.), *Means and ends in education* (Occasional Papers 2). Toronto: The Ontario Institute for Studies in Education, 1969.

Glaser, R. Individuals and learning: Adaptation or selection. Presidential address presented at the annual meeting of the American Educational Research Association, Chicago, 1972.

Goodnow, J. J. Rules and repertoires, rituals and tricks of the trade: Social and cognitive factors in the growth of ideas and representations. Unpublished manuscript. Washington, D. C.: The George Washington University, 1971

Humphreys, L. G. The humanistic movement in psychology and education: Some reservations. *The Science Teacher,* 1971, 38.

Irwin, M. H. A developmental study of elaboration modality effects in paired-associate learning. Unpublished doctoral dissertation. Berkeley: University of California, 1971.

Jensen, A. R. How much can we boost IQ and scholastic achievement? *Harvard Educational Review,* 1969, 39, 1–123.

————. Do schools cheat minority children? *Educational Researcher,* 1971, 14, 3–28.

Lambert, N. M. Paired associate learning, social status and tests of logical concrete behavior as univariate and multivariate predictors of first-grade reading achievement. *American Educational Research Journal,* 1970, 7, 511–528.

Resnick, L. B., Wang, M. C., and Kaplan, J. Behavior analysis in curriculum design: A hierarchically sequenced introductory mathematics curriculum. Monograph 2, Learning Research and Development Center, University of Pittsburgh, 1970.

Rohwer, W. D., Jr. Constraint, syntax, and meaning in paired-associate learning. *Journal of Verbal Learning and Verbal Behavior,* 1966, 5, 541–547.

————. Social class differences in the role of linguistic structures in paired-associate learning: Elaboration and learning proficiency. Final report on U. S. Office of Education Basic Research Project No. 5–0605, Contract No. OE 6–10–273. November, 1967.

————. Mental mnemonics in early learning. *Teachers College Record,* 1968, 70, 213–226.

————. Prime time for education: Early childhood or adolescence? *Harvard Educational Review,* 1971, 41, 316–341.

————. Learning and conceptual development in childhood and adolescence. In

H. W. Reese (Ed.), *Advances in child development and behavior.* New York: Academic Press, in press.

——, and Ammon, M. S. Elaboration training and learning efficiency in children. *Journal of Educational Psychology,* 1971, *62,* 376–383.

——, and Levin, J. R. Learning efficiency and elaboration training among four- and five-year-old children. In W. D. Rohwer, Jr., and P. R. Ammon. The assessment and improvement of learning and language skills in four- and five-year-old culturally disadvantaged children. Final report on Office of Economic Opportunity Contract Number OEO B99–4776. 1971.

——, Suzuki, N., and Levin, J. R. Population differences and learning proficiency. *Journal of Educational Psychology,* 1971, *62,* 1–14.

——, and Levin, J. R. Elaboration preferences and differences in learning proficiency. In J. Hellmuth (Ed.), *Cognitive studies: Deficits in cognition.* Volume 2. New York: Brunner/Mazel, Inc., 1971.

Weikart, D. P. Early childhood special education for intellectually subnormal and/or culturally different children. Paper prepared for the National Leadership Institute in Early Childhood Development in Washington, D. C., 1971.

Wolff, P., and Levin, J. R. The role of overt activity in children's imagery production. *Child Development,* in press.

# 6

# The Instructional Environment and the Young Autonomous Learner [1]

## EVAN R. KEISLAR

It is an old notion that learning proceeds best when the student takes the initiative in setting his goals and pursuing his education in ways that makes sense to him. Rousseau's *Emile* learned his lessons from nature itself, a theme of self-directed education, reflected by Pestalozzi and Froebel, which found one form of expression in the progressive education movement launched by John Dewey. In fact, some of the so-called experimental schools responded to the concept of child interest and demand to such an extreme that it called forth criticism from Dewey himself.

Thoughtful educators have sought to foster the growing independence of their students as learners and though their approaches varied widely, there appear to have been notable succeses for reasons we do not understand. In recent years, a whole host of factors within different cultural and philosophical frameworks have led to varied expressions of this idea under labels such as "individualized instruction," "the free school," "open structure," or "learner-controlled education." A common theme in all of these approaches is that of autonomy, the recognition that the learner exerts his own control over the instructional process.

At a philosophical level, of course, there is considerable debate on the question of autonomy. Skinner (1971) in his hotly discussed recent book, *Beyond Freedom and Dignity*, has stated in no uncertain terms that in the final analysis there is no such thing as autonomy. He equates this concept

[1] This study was carried out through the UCLA Center for Research in Early Childhood Education, sponsored by the United States Office of Economic Opportunity, Contract No. CG 9938, Dr. Carolyn Stern, Director.

124

with the superstitious idea of the homunculus in man. Since everything we do and are may be traced back to antecedent events, the concept that man can make his own decisions in the sense of being really free to do so is meaningless. For Carl Rogers (1969), the fact that man is both free to choose and still bound by determinism is accepted as a paradox—one that we must learn to live with. Other writers who have joined the fray include a variety of hostile critics such as Toynbee and Chomsky. John Platt (1972), in his cogent effort to reconcile the conflict between Skinner and the humanistic school, regards these two points of view as two sides of a coin. Platt concludes his review by saying, "For the solutions of our deep problems, in the long run, Skinner's manifesto is the only hope we have." If Jensen crystallized the issue for the Sixties, Skinner's *Beyond Freedom* may well be the issue of the Seventies.

At a practical classroom level, we may define the autonomous learner as one who makes the decisions relating to his own learning process. He decides what he will learn, how he will learn it, and when he will turn to other pursuits. Although in every classroom some form and degree of autonomy is permitted the learner, the variation is enormous. At one extreme, learners are given only limited opportunities to be autonomous, by selecting a topic for a paper or studying the required assignment in their own way. At the other extreme, the only constraints placed upon the learner are those of safety (for himself and his peers) and limits protecting the rights of others.

For many writers the feature of learner independence is a goal to be sought in and of itself; it represents a basic assumption about human existence. For others, learner-controlled instruction is defended because it is, in practice, more effective in the attainment of broad outcomes. Where specific outcomes are at stake, the research literature is unclear as to what learner control of the instructional process is desirable. Such ambiguity is understandable simply because of the host of factors which are necessarily involved.

Part of the problem hinges on the inadequacy of the definition proposed. How can we ever tell when a learner makes his own decisions in school? Some years ago on the opening day in September, a fourth-grade teacher in a progressive school designed the classroom so that, when the children arrived, they found over in one corner a set of musical instruments from Mexico; elsewhere was spread out a variety of Mexican costumes for the children to try on; in another corner a display of metal handicrafts from Mexico was carefully arranged; and on the back wall was a sample of breath-taking pictures of beautiful Mexican scenery, village life, and growing cities. On arrival the children had a marvelous time for a good 15 minutes, banging on drums, trying on costumes, playing the musical instruments, fingering the handicrafts, and gazing at the beautiful pictures. At the end of this period the teacher assembled the class and, after they had finally quieted down, said, "Well, this is a democratic classroom. What would you like to study this fall?" The vote was unanimous. It is difficult to ascertain whether the children or the teacher, or both, made the decision.

It does seem obvious that where the learner is offered no alternatives he is not likely to be making his own decisions. Nor can we be satisfied with a stacked set of choices from which to choose. Harold Carter, at the University of California, Berkeley, told the story, years ago, that he had discovered an excellent way to get his son to eat his cereal. He would pose the question brightly in the morning, "Do you want to have your cereal in the red bowl or the green bowl?" The young man was so preoccupied with these alternatives that he failed to consider the third possibility of no cereal at all.

While the learner must be given a genuine range of real options, such choices cannot be infinite and teacher influence in the selection is inevitable. To say that the environment must be a natural one, the real world, such as the school without walls, is an exciting point of view; but it does not solve this problem. Teachers, no matter how nondirective they wish to be, still influence their students and have something to do with the way students' decisions are made. Any discussion of the autonomous learner must deal with the nature of the educational setting.

One of the most valuable ways of describing the instructional environment, from the point of view of research, has been the model proposed originally, I believe, by Robert Glaser (1962) and discussed in detail by him in Chapter 4 of this volume. The model involves first setting objectives; second, assessing the present state of the learner; third, devising an instructional sequence; and, finally, evaluating the outcome. This four-fold set of categories is extremely flexible and has found a wide range of applications. One adaptation for the autonomous learner is presented in Figure 1. Across the top of this diagram are presented in modified form the four steps of Glaser's instructional model, with the learner presented as the decision-maker. Although this reflects a problem-solving framework, it includes the possibility of learning as a result of unplanned exploration or as an unintended product of other goal-directed activity. Teachers hope that the production activity involved in building a teepee, putting out a newspaper, or handing in a term paper is evidence of learning.

The role of the teacher is reflected in the lower set of boxes in Figure 1, which are focused upon the environmental resources necessary to provide the richness of opportunity for the learner. An important part of such resources is the opportunity to learn to make better decisions. Teachers frequently resist giving pupils the freedom to choose their own instructional goals because they fear that the child is unable to make "wise choices." By offering better opportunities to learn the consequences of different options, for example, children's decisions about goals may be more mature.

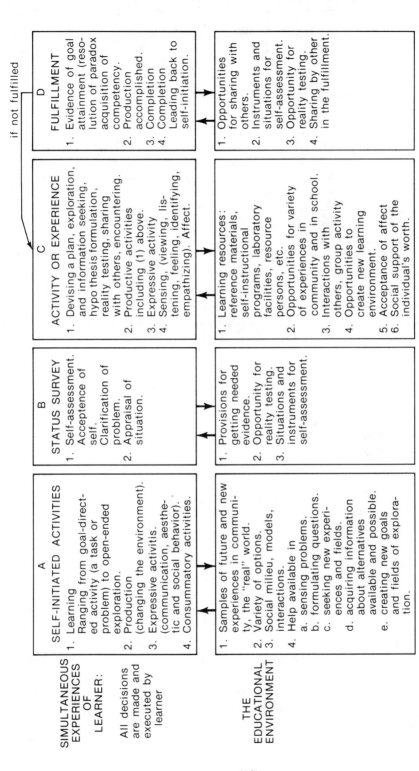

Figure 1. A working diagram of the relationships between the educational environment and the autonomous learner.

if not fulfilled

**SIMULTANEOUS EXPERIENCES OF LEARNER:**

All decisions are made and executed by learner

**THE EDUCATIONAL ENVIRONMENT**

**A**
**SELF-INITIATED ACTIVITIES**

1. Learning Ranging from goal-directed activity (a task or problem) to open-ended exploration.
2. Production (changing the environment).
3. Expressive activitis. (communication, aesthetic and social behavior).
4. Consummatory activities.

1. Samples of future and new experiences in community, the "real" world.
2. Variety of options.
3. Social milieu, models, interactions.
4. Help available in
   a. sensing problems.
   b. formulating questions.
   c. seeking new experiences and fields.
   d. acquiring information about alternatives available and possible.
   e. creating new goals and fields of exploration.

**B**
**STATUS SURVEY**

1. Self-assessment. Acceptance of self. Clarification of problem.
2. Appraisal of situation.

1. Provisions for getting needed evidence.
2. Opportunity for reality testing.
3. Situations and instruments for self-assessment.

**C**
**ACTIVITY OR EXPERIENCE**

1. Devising a plan, exploration, and information seeking, hypo thesis formulation, reality testing, sharing with others, encountering.
2. Productive activities including (1) above.
3. Expressive activity
4. Sensing, (viewing, listening, feeling, identifying, empathizing). Affect.

1. Learning resources: reference materials, self-instructional programs, laboratory facilities, resource persons, etc.
2. Opportunities for variety of experiences in community and in school.
3. Interactions with others, group activity
4. Opportunities to create new learning environment.
5. Acceptance of affect
6. Social support of the individual's worth.

**D**
**FULFILLMENT**

1. Evidence of goal attainment (resolution of paradox acquisition of competency.
2. Production accomplished.
3. Completion
4. Completion Leading back to self-initiation.

1. Opportunities for sharing with others.
2. Instruments and situations for self-assessment.
3. Opportunity for reality testing.
4. Sharing by other in the fulfillment.

127

## THE INSTRUCTIONAL ENVIRONMENT
## OF THE YOUNG LEARNER

The instructional point of view expressed in Figure 1 is highly congruent with the practices found in most preschools. In fact, it has been frequently pointed out that changes in the elementary school (e.g., the emergence of the British Primary School) have been strongly influenced by the institution of the preschool. The study of the autonomous learner and the instructional environment may be particularly valuable at a young age where the impact of formal school experience is absent.

From the standpoint of instructional research, it is important that summative evaluations be carried out to assess long-range programs involving different degrees of learner control. The evaluation of Planned Variations represents such an approach which is currently underway at the Head Start level. It is even more important, however, to study the various components of instruction to discover how the best program may be improved. Yet it is difficult to isolate for separate experimental study individual features of the open instructional environment where, in the interplay of a host of factors, the usual experimental controls are absent. The most important and complex variable, the teacher, has been the object of considerable study particularly at the descriptive level. Recently, for example, Resnick (1971) fruitfully recorded and analyzed the verbal behaviors of teachers in the British Primary School during sample periods of the school day. Less significant, but more amenable to experimental study are the material resources in the environment.

A global assessment of the value of the instructional materials in the classroom has not been greatly encouraging. Busse and his associates (1970) tested the effect of enriching the physical environment with about one hundred Head Start children who were randomly assigned to control and experimental classes. In each of the experimental classrooms was placed $1,300 worth of equipment including such things as tape recorders, farm animals, magnets, wooden puzzles, record sets, dolls, puppets, and so forth. Observation of the two groups of classes revealed no differences in the way in which teachers interacted with the children or the encouragement given children to use the available materials. However, the control children were as likely to be superior as the experimental, providing no support for the notion that simply enriching the environment through more materials has any value.

It is probably more fruitful to study small segments of the instructional environment. One promising component is the learning center. Here the young child encounters a set of materials in one part of the classroom. Hopefully, these are appealing and designed more or less as a unit. An essential feature is the fact that the child may choose whether or how much to play at the learning center, and that he may undertake the activity "on his own." Where an adult creates the interest center, it represents the independent variable; of course children frequently modify existing interest centers or create new ones of their own. The dependent variables are reflected in the way children react to such centers and the resultant learning outcomes.

From the point of view of instructional research, the learning center is analogous, therefore, to an instructional program. For example, to teach the concept of diagonality, Olson (1970) introduced apparatus into the classroom environment of the young child. The preschoolers were free to play with the materials as they chose during the school year. At the end of this period, these youngsters, in comparison with control children, showed a superior grasp of the concept.

It is desirable that the child encounter learning centers which vary in a multitude of ways. (See *Learning Centers: Children on Their Own*, Association for Childhood Education International, 1970, Washington, D. C.) One important dimension is the extent to which the center sets a problem for the child as compared to an open-ended activity. For example, play materials, such as painting or blocks, offer an infinite variety of options where no specific goal is presented. Such open-ended activity permits a wide range of novel responses. On the other hand, the didactic Montessori materials tend to pose problems geared to the maturity level of the child, who is able to determine for himself whether or not he has attained the appropriate solution.

## THE GENERAL PROBLEM

This general framework for conceptualizing the process of autonomous learning within a research strategy, has been applied to a number of studies carried out at the UCLA Early Childhood Research Center. The focus has been upon young learners, four- and five-year-old children in Head Start classes. These explorations represent an attempt to view different aspects of the way young children relate to one instructional resource. All of these investigations, successes and fiascos alike, have contributed helpful insights.

Our program has focused upon the study of goal-directed learning through the design of components in the environment. Particular emphasis has been given to the way the child, on his own, uses informational resources to attain an educational goal, i.e., the question of how children seek and use available information. The approach involved methods more like those of formative evaluation than classical experimental design. The data-gathering procedures ranged from the development and use of fairly precise testing devices to informal observations of children's reactions.

The research strategy was to move back and forth from studies of the learning center in a controlled laboratory context to those in an open class-room environment. After the first version was tried out at a preschool center and revised, a more controlled laboratory study was undertaken. Then the center was moved into the classroom to note what happened under typical classroom conditions. With new questions raised, another laboratory study was called for before returning to the classroom once again. While the procedure sounds more organized than it has been, the plan of moving back and forth from laboratory to classroom has seemed helpful.

Three types of questions were raised in studying this interface between the child and the instructional environment:

1. *Children's strategies of information-seeking and use.* How do children go about using an information source for their own self-instruction? What self-management skills or learning strategies are effective? Are such strategies a function of individual personality variables such as independence or achievement motivation? To what extent do peers act as a source of information?
2. *Effectiveness of the learning center in terms of immediate learning outcomes.* How much is learned in terms of the instructional goal, by what proportion of pupils? How much is the activity at the learning center enjoyed or preferred?
3. *Possible long-range outcomes.* Are experiences at the learning center likely to foster development in self-reliance and independence in learning? On this last question we can offer some speculations but little data.

## THE MEASUREMENT OF PREFERENCE
## FOR SCHOOL ACTIVITIES

It is difficult in a laboratory setting to estimate the extent to which children like or enjoy what it is they are doing in the experiment. Those of us who have taken subjects out of a classroom for our studies are pleased every time we enter the room and hear the voices of half a dozen children asking to be next. However, it is even more important to find out if the children who have already been included want to come back again. Apart from the uneasy feeling that the vocal few are not representative of the class, we also wonder whether this apparent enthusiasm reflects the child's desire to escape from an uninteresting classroom activity.

The importance of providing instructional resources which children will voluntarily seek and use has caused us to pay a good deal of attention to the problem of measuring the child's preference for activities in school. What is needed is a simple, easy-to-administer instrument. Of course, the most valid test would be the extent to which children actually relate to materials in a free classroom setting; but getting this information requires procedures which are too time-consuming for the developmental phase of a learning center.

We have explored a number of methods for obtaining a systematic measure of preference of activities with young children (Keislar, 1971). In one study we tried out a distancing technique based on an approach-avoidance concept, illustrated by a child pushing away a food he doesn't like. If children enjoy an activity, presumably it is one that they would approach. Pictures of activities drawn on cards were placed upright on a stand. The child was asked to arrange these in front of him in any way he chose, putting some farther, some closer. We hoped that he would put the activities he preferred physically close to him and others farther away. But the procedure did not work. Children placed the pictures either equidistant or at random. There was no consistency in their placements.

We were somewhat more successful when we asked the child to position three pictures in terms of a rating scale, the one he liked best close to him and the one he didn't like farthest away, but there was little evidence that the child was indicating his preferences in any reliable fashion.

The final form of the preference test was an adaptation of one developed in an earlier study (Keislar and McNeil, 1960). Using a paired-comparison technique, the child is presented with a succession of pairs of pictures, each one showing a child engaged in a familiar school activity. Separate forms have been developed for each sex. As each pair of pictures is shown to the child, he is asked, for example, "Do you like to play with blocks or do you like to play with toys? Point to what you like to do best."

The test has been "standardized" in such a way that it is possible to assess the preference for any new activity which may be involved in an investigation. In this case, the new procedure is compared with five standard activities, which are generally found in schools: playing with blocks, looking at picture books, painting, playing with toys (cars and dolls), and assembling puzzles. The preference scores range therefore from 0 to a maximum of 5, depending on how many times the new activity was preferred over the standard ones. To save time in administering this preference test, we have used eight pairs of pictures, omitting several pairs which compared two of the standard activities.

In order to find out whether Head Start youngsters were indicating their "real" preference with such an instrument, a validity study was conducted. Twenty-eight Head Start children were given the paired-comparison test, involving only the five standard activities. The child was then led to one side of the room where the materials needed for each of these activities had been previously placed behind screens. The materials were borrowed from the child's own classroom. The screens for two activities, the one most preferred by the child and one least preferred, were then removed. The child was invited to play with one of these activities for a "little while" before returning to his class. All youngsters readily selected an activity and stayed to play. How well did the picture preference test predict the actual choice? In 75 percent of the cases, this figure was interpreted as indicating an acceptable level of validity for the rest.

## INFORMATION-SEEKING

Although many learning centers offer a medium for expression and a fulfillment of many social and personal needs, other centers in the classroom are important because they offer the young child an opportunity for exploration and consequent contact with an information-rich environment. The child acquires not only specific information in this way but he "learns to learn" through the cultivation of covert attentional habits and a variety of self-management skills.

A child's exploratory activity at a learning center may reflect the competence motive of White (1959) or the "will to learn" proposed by Logan (1972). At some centers, such exploration may simply be referred to as curiosity, to follow Berlyne's suggestion (1960), since it does not appear related to any goal. On the other hand, where a particular instructional task is posed by the center, the child engages in purposeful information-seeking activities. Following the formulation in Figure 1, the center should provide appropriate resources to permit this self-instruction to proceed.

As part of his growing competence in information-seeking, the child learns to recognize when he needs information, to seek it out, and to use it for the attainment of his goals. When the information source has served its purpose, hopefully he discards it. A learning center should be designed to facilitate this growth in learning abilities. Informal observations of children during such self-instruction have suggested, however, that children make two types of errors. Some adopt a trial-and-error strategy, making little use of available information; they act as if they hope to win by luck. Others appear to rely too much on the information source in what seems to be an over-cautious pattern of behavior.

In an earlier study, these two types of errors appeared where kindergarten children sought and used information in teaching themselves to speak French (Bland and Keislar, 1966). The subjects learned to describe pictures drawn on Language Master cards by saying appropriate French sentences (formed by using one each of five nouns, five adjectives, and five predicates). By playing a card on the Language Master, each child could hear the correct sentence for the picture on that card. In this way it was possible for each child to obtain information whenever he wanted it. The criterion test consisted of pictures which the child had not seen before but which were to be described by sentences involving new combinations of the words he had learned. Most of the children learned to speak a good deal of French in this way. However, even after one recognizes variations in rate of learning, there appeared to be large differences in the extent to which the Language Master cards were used.

Over-reliance on an information source may be viewed as a form of self-prompting to an extreme. In a now classic study, Gates (1917) showed the inefficiency of over-prompting for the learning of factual materials. More recent work in programmed instruction (Anderson, Faust, and Roderick, 1968; Markle, 1969) provide similar conclusions.

On the other hand, failing to take advantage of available information may mean excessive use of trial and error, a strategy likely to be adopted by younger children (Munn, 1954). It is of interest to note that Weir (1964) found that where only the simplest strategy was appropriate younger children did better than older. Kagan and his associates (1964) have pointed out that the impulsive child, who is more likely to adopt a trial-and-error approach, is going to face failure far more often.

## THE LEARNING CENTER: THE ANIMAL GAME

In designing a learning center as the independent variable for study, a number of criteria were adopted: (1) The center must offer children a clear instructional goal; it must supply evidence that the learner is making progress toward that goal. (2) The center must appeal to most young children so that, without special encouragement, they will initiate activities at the center. (3) What the child does while manipulating materials must be sufficient to maintain motivation to demonstrate learning; extrinsic sources of reinforcement such as teacher approval should not be necessary. (4) The center must provide children with opportunities to make decisions about their own instructional processes, such as control of sequence, seeking information, and self-evaluation. (5) There should be an opportunity for the learner to adjust the difficulty of the tasks and subtasks. (6) The center should require no monitoring on the part of the teacher. It should be a self-contained independent area of the classroom.

With a simple goal the child is likely to be more aware of what is called for and the child's self-instructional processes are more easily observed. Consequently, the major unit used for the studies was a learning center which posed a paired-associate learning task. This associative learning is not unlike much of what is included in the preschool curriculum. For example, such outcomes constitute a large part of the preschool television program, "Sesame Street."

The instructional goal for the center was to learn where each of nine animals lived by matching a picture of the animal with a picture of its habitat. For example, when a child was faced with a picture of a seal, he picked a picture of a rocky ocean coastline; for a monkey, he picked a jungle scene. This task both appealed to children of this age and is not ordinarily taught as part of the preschool curriculum. With very few exceptions, on the pretest Head Start children performed only slightly above chance.

The apparatus consisted of a wooden box with a sloping top, a set of nine animal pictures, and a reference book. The habitat pictures were mounted on the top of the box in three rows, three pictures per row. At the bottom of each habitat picture was a keyed slot into which could be inserted any of the nine cards, but only to the depth of one-quarter inch. Keyed strips on the back of the cards permitted only the correct animal picture to pass through the slot for a habitat. When the child had put all the animals where they lived, he could retrieve the cards by pulling open a door at the front of the box and play the game again.

To permit the child to seek and obtain the information he needed for this activity, a picture reference book was placed on a stand beside the game box. Nine reference tabs at the side of the book, each one showing a picture of the animals, permitted the child to look up the habitat of the animal and thus prompt himself whenever he wished. When he pulled a tab to open the book, he found the corresponding picture of a habitat. Thus, by simply matching the pictures he could place each animal card in the proper habitat slot. This idea of "looking up" something in a book was a new one for the youngsters; consequently a separate, much more simple, task was developed as a preliminary game to help the children learn how to use such a reference source. In this orientation, pictures of different animals and a corresponding different reference book were involved.

## EFFECTIVENESS OF A TRIAL-AND-ERROR STRATEGY

A laboratory study was first conducted to see whether four- and five-year-old Head Start children could use these reference materials to learn effectively (Keislar and Phinney, in press). It was hoped that the youngsters would move from chance performance on the pretest to a 90 percent criterion, one error or less on the posttest. It was also hoped that the game would be sufficiently interesting to young children so that, on the picture paired-comparison preference test previously described, they would select the experimental activity more often than most of the standard activities presented.

In addition to the critical question as to whether children could easily learn to use this reference book system as a source of information in mastering these paired associates was the question of whether children could learn just as well by using a simple trial-and-error method. Since the apparatus described permitted knowledge of results, it was not inconceivable that children could learn by simply trying each card in one slot after another. We wanted to make sure that children were not rewarded for resorting to this strategy.

Fourteen Head Start children, randomly assigned to two groups, came individually to a room adjacent to their class for a daily session lasting about 10 to 12 minutes over a three-day period. The trial-and-error group had no access to the reference book but were encouraged to use the knowledge of results from each try. The information-seeking group were shown how to use the information source which was at first required, then made optional and, for the final round, removed.

The results showed clearly that the trial-and-error strategy was fairly ineffective. Although posttest performance of the group was definitely above chance levels ($M = 5.6$ out of a possible 9), it did not approach the almost perfect performance of the group which used the reference book on a gradually fading basis ($M = 8.4$). On the preference test, most of these subjects rated the activity as their first or second choice out of the six activities presented. As might be expected, one apparent reason for the poor performance of the trial-and-error group was simply that they spent less time looking at the pictures (something which the information-seeking group had to do to locate and use the information available) and more time "hunting" for the right slot.

## USING INCENTIVES TO OPTIMIZE
## AN INFORMATION-SEEKING STATEGY

Observations of children playing the animal game revealed the usual wide range of individual differences in reliance on the information source. Although there was no conclusive evidence that children were making such errors, it appeared that some were relying entirely too much on the book and were thus overprompting themselves while others were using excessive amounts of trial and error and thus underprompting. It was hoped, of course, that children using such materials would be encouraged to avoid wild guessing but would be willing to make a try when reasonable mastery had been attained. It seemed plausible that heightening the incentive to reduce such extreme behavior would foster more effective learning.

Ten Head Start children participated in this next experiment. Each child came in for an individual session once a day for three days. Following procedures found to be effective in earlier studies (cf. Keislar, 1960; Lipe and Jung, 1971), marbles were used as incentives. For each reinforcing event, the child received a marble which he placed in a tray in front of him. As he played, the marbles he received thus formed a bar graph to remind him of his growing success. To avoid a policy of giving prizes, the children were told that they could not keep the marbles.

Half of the children, the experimental group, were differentially reinforced only when they placed the card correctly on their first try without using the reference book; this performance was precisely the same behavior called for on the posttest. Every child earned at least one and usually several marbles on each round of the game. The children in the control group were indiscriminately reinforced; they received a marble when each card was correctly placed regardless of what they did to get it there. Theoretically, a child in the control group could get reinforced consistently without learning anything.

The results showed, quite contrary to our expectations, that the control group ($M = 8.0$) did significantly better than the experimental ($M = 4.6$). The use of special incentives had failed in producing better learning. How did the youngsters in this study use the reference book? Subjects in both groups showed a decreasing reliance on the book; in other words, they were indeed fading their own prompts (see Figure 2). However, the experimental group, if anything, seems to have used the book slightly more than the control. It is clear that there is no support for the hypothesis that placing a premium on becoming independent of the information source weaned these youngsters from the reference book any faster. It is also of interest to note that the standard deviation in the use of the reference book was more than three times as large for the experimental group than for the control.

The second study clearly indicates that providing extrinsic incentives was

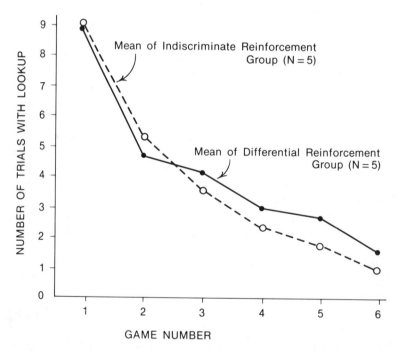

Figure 2. *Mean number of trials per game where reference was looked up for two groups.*

ineffective, in fact, even damaging to learning. One plausible explanation of this reversed finding was that the children in the differential reinforcement group were clearly under greater pressure to learn rapidly and do well; risks were involved. The challenge affected the children differently. For the group as a whole the interfering effects of this risk situation may have been relatively large. On the other hand, the children in the indiscriminate reinforcement group, in a more secure and rewarding atmosphere, may have been better able to attend to the task. It was concluded that the individual reactions to external motivating conditions differ so much that it may be better to let the child judge how much to rely on the book!

## THE CLASSOOM SETTING

With some assurance that the procedures were effective and that the activities held some appeal, the learning center was placed in an open classroom setting. The main problem was simply to find out how much, if at all, children would learn when given the opportunity to play the game under minimal controls. The animal game was therefore placed successively in three different Head Start classes in East Los Angeles for four days each. Teachers were requested to treat this center just like any of the other sets of materials in the classroom with one exception: they were not to coach the children on the task. Otherwise, no constraints were placed on how the children would use the materials.

In these studies, all efforts were made to keep things as natural as possible by reducing all external influences to a minimum. Nevertheless, the conduct of the research demanded some interference. Since it seemed necessary to find out how much these youngsters knew about the task before contact with the learning center, pretests were given to two of the classes. In the third classroom, however, to eliminate the possible effect of such a test experience prior to the "treatment," no pretest was given. Furthermore, to avoid the possibility that children would "play up" to an observer, in two of the classrooms no systematic observations were made; instead, an assistant dropped in occasionally just to make sure that things were going along smoothly during the four-day period. In the third classroom, however, an observer was constantly present to keep a record of everything that went on. On one occasion, pictures were taken in this room. There was no evidence, however, that the presence of the observer made any difference.

The necessity for orientation was also a problem in the attempt to study the learning center under "natural" classroom conditions. We had found that without some kind of orientation on the use of the reference book, Head Start children would rely on trial and error. Yet, we wanted to hold such external instruction to a minimum. The compromise solution was to provide orientation for a small proportion of the group, hoping that the rest would learn what to do from the initiated minority. The orientation game, as previously described, was given to one-third of the youngsters before being introduced into the classroom. In spite of our efforts to obtain a random sample from this Mexican-American population, somehow the youngsters present at orientation were better at speaking English than the rest of the sample and performed slightly better on the pretest. Although we were probably fortunate in having better communication during orientation, our conclusion about the value of orientation is confounded. Oriented youngsters showed slightly higher scores on the posttest, but we can not be sure why.

In the one monitored classroom, the game was in constant use during the first two days and used 90 percent of the time during the last two. As would be expected, wide individual differences in participation were found; although the average child played the game five times (taking a total of 17 minutes), some never played and one played ten times.

Test results for the three classes, shown in Figure 3, are based on all children regardless of their participation. The available pretest scores average slightly above chance. It should be noted that while the posttest means of the three classes are all between 5.5 and 6.0, approximately one-third of the youngsters in each class reached the criterion of no more than one error. Because the children interacted freely with each other, the classroom is the appropriate experimental unit. Since this leaves an N of 3, no statistical tests were conducted. It appears, however, that a large proportion of children in each class showed evidence of learning to a high criterion.

How did the children use the reference book in this uncontrolled free situation? In our laboratory study there was a consistent decrease in the use of the book across six rounds (Figure 2). The children in the observed classroom played the game in an average of five rounds. Did they use the book less and less as they learned? Since different children played different numbers of rounds, to answer this question a Vincent curve was constructed. The graph indicated little evidence that on the average these children were "fading the prompt" under these conditions, although a few youngsters seemed to rely on the book sparingly. Some children who played even five to ten times used the book heavily throughout; they seemed simply to enjoy turning the pages and looking up the animals. The materials were being used for something more than mastering the task the experimenter had in mind!

## INDIVIDUAL DIFFERENCES IN STYLE
## OF INFORMATION-SEEKING

The puzzling differences in the way in which children sought or did not seek information from the reference book led to a number of speculations similar to those offered in explanation of the results of the incentive study reported earlier. Was the anxious, dependent child relying heavily on the

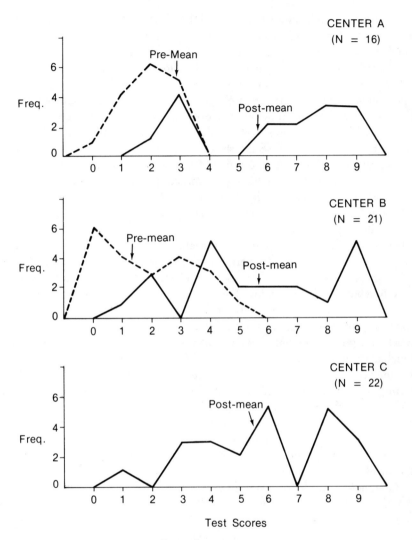

*Figure 3. Pre- and posttest distributions of scores at three Head Start centers where animal game was left in room for four days.*

reference book and thus, by making the task easier, avoiding failure? Was it the fast-responding, impulsive child who rarely sought to use the book and presumably counted on luck to accomplish the task? Did the high achievement-motivated youngster, as the literature suggests, make the task into a challenging one of moderate difficulty by using the book only when he seemed to require it? Answers to these questions would be helpful in designing effective learning centers.

Previous research suggests the plausibility of the hypotheses posed by these questions. For example, Gratch (1964) found that dependent children, as rated by their teachers, make the same kind of guesses on a task as independent children, but are much less willing to wager on their guesses. Kagan (1966) has identified a behavior syndrome for the impulsive child, the youngster who acts quickly without carefully reflecting on the alternatives. A wide range of literature also suggests that even among young children differences in achievement motivation may be observed; children differ reliably in the extent to which they will seek tasks of intermediate difficulty where there is a moderate risk of success and failure (cf. Crandall 1969; Veroff, 1969).

In our next study, in which 20 children played the game individually under laboratory conditions, the focus was upon the development of measures related to the strategy of information-seeking and use. A critical factor seemed to be how much a child was willing to play his hunches. In other words, when a subject was not completely certain about where to place a card, to what extent did he seek information to assist him instead of taking a chance?

In simply observing children use the reference source, it is difficult to tell exactly what the child is doing. For example, it is not clear whether children are using the book in spite of the fact that they are practically sure of the right answer or because they are completely uncertain. Neither can one tell whether a guess represents a wild shot in the dark or a highly informed reasonable choice. Since these young children were unable to verbalize the judgments about their own growing competence, it is desirable to obtain during the playing of the game additional information on how well the child has learned the material. Such information does not, of course, give the complete story; a child may genuinely believe he knows the answer when in fact he may be in total ignorance and vice versa. Nevertheless, evidence regarding the child's growing competence is essential in interpreting his behavior of using the reference book.

One method we had previously explored was to have the child play under two different alternating conditions. When a green sign was displayed above the box, the child was allowed to use the book at his option; after two or three such rounds, a red card was shown instead, meaning that the resource book was now unavailable for use. After one "red" round, which essentially constituted a test, the green card was restored. However, the procedure was judged to provide too rough an estimate of competence, since knowledge of results was constantly available during the test, a child's competence could change before the following round.

A two-step technique, involving a slight apparatus change, was finally adopted. Each child first made a "guess" as to where the animal card belonged by resting the card in the slot in front of the chosen habitat. He could then decide whether to look up the information and perhaps change his guess. When he decided to confirm his choice he pulled a ring at the front of the box; if he had chosen the correct slot the card dropped through. The procedure provided some estimate of the child's learning at each step without giving knowledge of results.

The use of such a two-step procedure permitted the calculation of two kinds of scores to describe styles of information-seeking. Both of these scores were based on what the learner did after he made a guess, but before he found out whether his guess was right or wrong. (1) *Book-reliance* was measured by the proportion of times the book was used when the guess was correct. High scores on this measure would suggest over-prompting. (2) *Chance-taking*, how much the child was willing to gamble, was measured by the proportion of times that he failed to use the book when his guess was incorrect. High scores here are indicative of under-prompting.

Three personality measures were obtained for each youngster. Latency was the average time taken by the child to make his initial guess for each card. Dependence was measured by the use of a teacher rating scale to assess such factors as anxiety, reluctance to face new situations, looking to the teacher for help. As a measure of achievement motivation, an adaptation of Veroff's test battery was devised.

The three questions originally posed led to the following predictions: (1) Dependent children would be likely to over-prompt themselves and thus show relatively high scores on the criterion of book-reliance. (2) Quick-responding, impulsive children would under-prompt and thus get relatively high scores on chance-taking. (3) Children whose achievement motivation is strong would prompt themselves only when the risk of being wrong was high; they would show low scores on both criteria.

The conduct of this study revealed that learning under these procedures was clearly more difficult for the children. Instead of taking only six games to master the task, this group required nine. Even then, as a group, their performance did not equal the almost perfect posttest scores of previous groups under laboratory conditions. Using a procedure similar to the one adopted here, Berlyne and associates (1968) also found that asking children first to offer a guess about each pair made the task of learning more difficult.

Unfortunately, the results showed that the distribution of the two criteria were highly skewed and the reliabilities low. After a guess was made, for most of the children in this group there was a strong tendency to check it out. Book-reliance scores piled up near zero while the chance-taking figures were up at the other extreme. Although there was no other way to assess over-prompting, a substitute measure was used for under-prompting. Chance-taking was estimated by the following procedure: After the child's first guess had been shown to be wrong, the proportion of times he tried again without using the book was noted. Although this measure may suffer from the fact that it may still reflect competence, it showed a high reliability of .90.

The children were highly consistent in the time they took to make their responses, the reliability of the measure of latency being .96. The reliabilities of the other two personality measures, dependence and achievement motivation, were not high enough to warrant their use. On the average a child took significantly less time to make a guess which was correct than one which was incorrect. There was a significant relationship between latency and the use of the book when the first guess was wrong ($r = .50$). This finding supports the notion that lack of reliance on the book is part of the impulsive syndrome. However, because of the limitation of the measure, we must hold it with a reservation. Subsequent efforts to improve these measures have been partially successful but further clarification of these variables is called for.


## PEERS AS RESOURCES FOR LEARNING

An important feature of the classroom, sometimes neglected in the preparation of instructional programs, is the presence of constant social interaction throughout a learning sequence. With the learning center, for example, children helped each other, took turns watching and playing, laughed and talked about many irrelevant things. Under these social circumstances the self-instructional behavior of the learners was undoubtedly very different from that observed in the individual laboratory settings. One function of vertical grouping, as in the British Primary School, is that older children are available to orient and assist their peers who may be two or three years younger. In the classroom tryouts of the learning center, this informal teaching function of peers was made use of by orienting only one-third of the class.

During recent years a good deal of interest has been expressed in tutoring, especially through formal procedures whereby older children from higher grades are assigned to work with children in lower grades. In such studies the focus of interest has usually been on the tutor. For example, Gartner and associates (1971) found that elementary school children who were being tutored enjoyed the sessions but did not show more than normal growth. It was the high school tutors who profited by making enormous gains in relatively short periods of time. Frager and Stern (1970) found similar values for cross-age tutoring at the elementary level. Feshbach and Devor (1969) studied the teaching styles of four-year-olds as they instructed three-year-olds. They found that children from middle-class families used positive reinforcements more than lower-class children.

In one laboratory study, we looked at the process of peer tutoring by four-year-olds with 16 Head Start children as subjects (Keislar and Blumenfeld, 1972). The structured curriculum, designed to teach prepositions, took the form of a matching game in which the learners identified the pictures described by their tutors and vice versa. The goal was to assess the effectiveness of the procedure by looking at the particular contribution of the tutors. It was possible that children could communicate effectively without ever using the prepositions for which the game was designed. Two groups of tutors were selected, four who knew the material, as demonstrated by their successful passing of a competency pretest, and four who failed the test. Their pupils, who had all failed, were assigned at random. The pairs played the game for four days, ten to 15 minutes per day.

The results supported the notion that to be a good teacher at the four-year-old level, a person should know his subject. On the other hand, there was evidence to suggest that this is not all; while three of the four pupils with competent tutors learned to a 90 percent criterion, one showed no gain at all. Why? Although her teacher was most qualified in the subject field, he was an arrogant young man who was utterly impatient with the slowness of his pupil's progress and who would vent his displeasure in no uncertain terms. The pupil not only learned nothing but, on the paired comparison preference test previously described, rated the activity at the very bottom of the list.

In the next classroom study, we paid particular attention to the way a child used his peers as a source of help instead of using the reference book. Peers act as a resource in two ways: (1) when the learner is the player, they may serve in a tutorial capacity as information sources, or, (2) with the learner simply watching, they may serve as models. A child therefore could master the task at the learning center without using the information source at all. With the experience of the pilot study of tutoring, we were also sensitive to the possible detrimental effect of peer interactions.

The animal game was placed in a large Head Start Center for six days. The posttest scores again were quite similar to earlier findings, about one-third of the class reaching a high criterion. The oriented one-third in this study scored only half a point higher on the posttest than did the nonoriented children.

The game was used each day from 70 to 100 percent of the time. On the large majority of rounds, more than one child was present in addition to the player. Sometimes there were as many as five or six. We had hoped to be able, on a card-by-card basis, to identify the source of help sought or received (with or without asking). However, the situation was too complex and we obtained information on a more gross, per-round, basis. Even here, it was impossible to tell whether the child was asking for help; he would often get it without asking for it, sometimes when it was clear he didn't want it.

The record of different types of social interactions during this six-day period is summarized in Figure 4. Using as the base the total number of rounds played by all children on a particular day, the graphs are plotted in terms of the percentage of this figure for each day in succession. For all days combined, on 58 percent of the rounds there was at least one other child present, sometimes as many as five or six. On 45 percent of the rounds, there was a

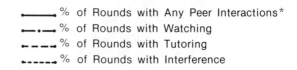

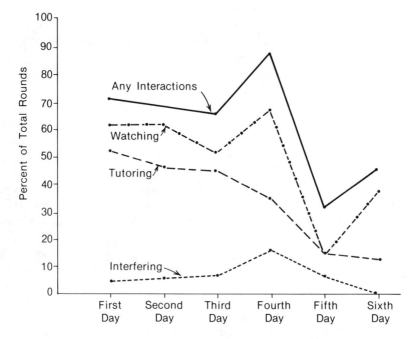

*Figure 4. Percent of total rounds on successive days with different types of peer interactions.*

* The total reflects only one interaction per round. Since it was possible to have all three types of interactions during any one round, the combined values are greater than the total number of rounds. The average number of children at the game, in addition to the player, on successive days was 1.9, 2.5, 1.4, 1.8, 1.1, and 1.3.

child watching and presumably learning from the activity of the player. Tutoring of one kind or another took place on 29 percent of the rounds. Lastly, on 11 percent of all the rounds the observer noted some kind of interference, that is, where the player clearly tried to discourage, either physically or verbally, an attempted intervention, however well-meaning, by a peer.

It seems likely that the overall impact of this learning center, in terms of posttest performance, is to a large extent accomplished by the fact that these four- and five-year-old youngsters learned from each other through being tutored or simply watching. Even through simply watching, without playing the game, many children may have learned much of what they later demonstrated.

Some of the informal anecdotal observations should be mentioned. We found that most children explored the box a good deal, sometimes putting two cards into it at once to see if this would work or trying to peek inside the box itself. Many youngsters seemed to enjoy finding pictures of the animals in the book as an activity in itself. Some matched the animal to the book instead of the procedure we expected. Since many children spoke Spanish at home, much Spanish was spoken as they worked. There was a good deal of verbalization such as, "I know where he lives," or "Aqui," "Abajo," as the lookers-on helped some player.

Children frequently resisted being taught. Sometimes when a peer would tell the player where a card went, the child would put the card down on the tray and select another one instead. One little boy who was waiting said, "When it's my turn, don't show me." One child who was shown by her friend where a card belonged still looked it up in the book apparently to verify it for herself. On occasion some children, when apparently they did not know where to put the animal, would sometimes open the book just a crack and peek into it as if, perhaps, this was verboten.

One particularly interesting child, Alice, was rated by teachers as the most withdrawn and shy youngster in the center, one often found in tears. She played the game a total of over 35 times in six days, an average of almost six times per day. Alice was a child who used the book constantly even after several days of playing. It was clear that the reference book no longer functioned as a teaching resource; many different personality and social needs were being met. However, the observer noted that during the latter part of the six-day period, Alice with her new-found competence was now interacting with the children more as she became a tutor, an activity which was to her a real source of satisfaction. In evaluating a learning resource, there are many outcomes which need to be considered.[2]

It is of interest to note some of the relationships which have been found in different studies of the learning center. While the number of cases in any class is too small to establish reliability, a number of correlations between .30 and .50 have stood up fairly well and are suggestive. Performance on the posttest is related to the total number of rounds played and to mental age on the Peabody Picture Vocabulary Test. Preference for the game on the Paired Comparison Preference Test, described earlier, is related both to posttest per-

[2] The incident is reminiscent of a frequently-observed nursery school phenomenon in which the insecure child for a large part of the morning is likely to end up on the swing, where he finds a less threatening social situation. Docia Zavitkovsky extended this illustration by pointing out that the same phenomenon may be observed among nursery school student teachers: at the beginning of the year the novice student teacher is likely to be found pushing children on the swings for most of the morning!

formance and to the average number of games played per day, suggesting further validity of this test.

## CONCLUDING DISCUSSION

The relation between the work of the educational researcher and the real world of the classroom has been a topic of considerable concern. Skinner, almost two decades ago, advanced the compelling thesis that the reason psychology has had so little impact on education was not because the laboratory is unlike a classroom but because the classroom does not look like a laboratory. Most of the ensuing work in programmed instruction reflected this point of view and attempted to reduce uncontrolled sources of error variance as much as possible by shrinking the domain of learner-made decisions. The result, in all too many cases, was a drab, dull experience for the learner which some researchers identified and called "the pall effect."

Since this early period, there has been considerable progress in the development of programs which are successful in maintaining the attention of learners beyond the initial stage of novelty. One trend has been to relax the criterion of control by offering far more options. Many programs, for example, offer a variety of shorter sequences or modules, so that pupils and teachers may select a more appropriate order in accordance with local demands. Even on a daily basis, a variety of activities are generally proposed to provide far more self-direction by the learner.

Studies which have attempted to assess the value of giving the learner options in instructional programs have usually failed to establish reliable differences (cf. Campbell and Chapman, 1967). Often the strange conclusion is reached that, since there is no demonstrated advantage to giving the learner greater control, it is the programmer who might just as well make the instructional decisions! However, overlooked in such research is the fact that permitting the learner to make his own decisions is meaningless if, with reasonable amounts of support, he may markedly improve his decision-making skill. The learner is not always given adequate information about the nature and consequences of the options, and he usually receives no appropriate instruction in learning how to choose. It is also likely that the question of learner control involves the critical matter of individual differences, variables such as those looked at in the studies just reviewed.

Questions of learner autonomy require consideration of both specific features of the environment and the resources the learner brings to the setting. Where the situation poses an instructional goal, a variety of self-instructional skills are important. At the Learning Research and Development Center at Pittsburgh a large number of specific self-management skills have been identified (Reynolds, 1971; Reynolds and Linehart, 1971), ranging from attention to task, self-evaluation, and self-prescription to problem-solving techniques such as seeking assistance from other materials, peers, or the teacher. A major outcome from such long-range programs may be the self-regulating behaviors which help the learner to profit more from his school environment. However, such skills are treated fairly closely within the context of the specific tasks encountered by the programs. It is not yet clear as to what extent broad, general strategies, to be used by autonomous learners, may be taught (cf. Keislar, 1970). There may be considerable promise, however, in programs designed to modify the motivational patterns of learners (Adkins *et al.*, 1971; DeCharms, 1972) so that the learner becomes more independent.

The self-management skill involved in the learning center reviewed in this chapter was information-seeking. Wide individual differences were found in the way young children engaged in self-prompting. Although no definitive evidence was obtained, it seems plausible that the way children attack this task of self-instruction reflects broader personality patterns. There was some support for a pattern of impulsivity in this task. Other findings, with low unreliable relationships, suggest the value of further exploration of the notion that children with high achievement motivation seek information in a more effective fashion than do either the anxious, dependent youngsters or their impulsive, quick-responding peers.

It seems most appropriate in designing goal-directed learning centers, that, among other things, a variety of task difficulties be presented. Children when given the option of doing so will seek out tasks commensurate with (1) their level of intellectual maturity (cf. Hunt's concept of match, 1961) and (2) their personality pattern in terms of such factors as impulsivity and achievement motivation. It is not clear, within an open framework, just what the nature of such a variety of task difficulties should be and how the child might be introduced and guided to use these resources most effectively for his own development. The design of the animal game learning center was such that the difficulty of the task could be altered at any time by the learner; the child was free to get help and look up at any time. This adjustable difficulty feature may be an important one to include in many learning centers.

In his discussions of the relation between basic laboratory research and the classroom, Glass (1971) maintains that educational research should give up the goal of trying to get teachers to apply general conclusions from basic studies. Using Rothkopf's mathemagenic model as an example, he points out that the results of carefully done studies are subject to a host of variables in a classroom setting, a fact which mitigates against any practical use unless the specific conditions of that situation have been studied. He concludes that the utilization of basic knowledge requires the generation of instructional materials with demonstrated value. It is through the vehicle of such artifacts that basic research can have an impact in the classroom.

The highly applied strategy adopted for the collection of studies reviewed here is one of moving back and forth from a controlled laboratory setting to the classroom. It permits a continuous close relationship between the restricted conditions of the research laboratory and the complex situation in the school setting. The vehicle for transfer between the two is a set of standardized and replicable materials whose features can be adapted and modified as called for. The approach offers the opportunity to gain a classroom perspective upon what is happening in the laboratory, and conversely, to study under controlled conditions items of interest noted in the classroom. It involves a combination of an experimental approach and an observational, descriptive study of both individuals and classes. Although there is a tendency, certainly apparent in this report, to look at too many different questions, the present illustration of the strategy underlines the problem of dealing in an analytic fashion with a component of the complex environment. Most of the studies simply raised questions for further exploration.

This investigation of the interface between an autonomous learner and instructional resources was focussed upon a single learning center, designed for the study of self-instructional behavior rather than for regular classroom use. Nevertheless, some perspective on broader issues may be gained by attempting to evaluate this small component, a week-long experience by young children. Although the issue is a complex one (cf. Kozol, 1972) it was assumed here that the child's autonomy is not infringed upon, if he is given the option of seeking goals deemed by others to contribute to significant objectives. Furthermore, teachers may demonstrate respect for the child's right to make his own decisions even though they openly present their views and values. An external evaluator is likely to use as criteria the two goals of the center in noting that (1) a third of the children mastered the associative learning task, a relatively minor objective, and (2) there was uncertain progress toward a much more important long-range goal, the acquisition of skills and attitudes of self-instruction which might contribute to the child's development as an independent learner. However, since there was some anecdotal evidence to suggest the possibility of other outcomes, such as social development and internal locus of control, a more adequate assessment of a longer instructional period should be conducted, possibly as a type of goal-free evaluation proposed by Michael Scriven.

A formative evaluation procedure involving careful study of the children's use of such a center may be more helpful in suggesting future directions than a purely summative assessment. Two criteria here are frequency of use (a question raised often in connection with libraries and playgrounds) and effectiveness. A goal-directed learning center, which is used little or in ways unlikely to aid a child to reach the goal, may need to be redesigned or replaced. However, as noted earlier, children frequently use a learning center quite effectively for ends not anticipated by the designers!

Although the present resource partially meets these two criteria, it is not clear how the center contributes to or interferes with other more significant goals. This third criterion involves a broad study of the variables involved. Present efforts were only partially successful in suggesting factors related to how much the center was used, in what ways, by what kinds of youngsters, and with what possible outcomes. However, there may be some promise in the strategy adopted, but not adequately realized, in studying children's use of such resources under both laboratory and classroom conditions.

## REFERENCES

Adkins, D. C., and Ballif, B. L. Preschool motivation curriculum. Center for Research in Early Childhood Education. University of Hawaii, 1971.

Anderson, R. C., Faust, G. W., and Roderick, M. C. Overprompting in programmed instruction. *Journal of Educational Psychology*, 1968, 59, 88–93.

Berlyne, D. C. *Conflict, arousal and curiosity.* New York: McGraw-Hill, 1960.

————, Carrey, S. T., Lazare, S. A., Parlow, J., and Tiberius, R. Effects of prior guessing on intentional and incidental paired-associate learning. *Journal of Verbal Learning*, 1968, 7, 750–759.

Bland, M., and Keislar, E. R. A self-controlled audio-lingual program for children. *The French Review*, 1966, 2, 266–276.

Busse, T. V., Ree, M., and Gutride, M. Environmentally enriched classrooms and the play of Negro preschool children. *Urban Education*, 1970, 5, 128–140.

Campbell, V., and Chapman, M. A. Learner control vs. program control of instruction. *Psychology in the Schools*, 1967, 4, 121–130.

Crandall, V. C. Sex differences in expectancy of intellectual and academic reinforcement. In Charles P. Smith (Ed.), *Achievement-related motives in children.* Russell Sage Foundation. New York, 1969.

De Charms, R. From pawns to origins: toward self-motivation. In G. S. Lesser (Ed.), *Psychology and educational practice.* Glenview, Illinois: Scott Foresman, 1971. Pp. 380–407.

Feshbach, N., and Devor, G. Teaching styles in four-year-olds. *Child Development*, 1969, 40, 183–190.

Fowler, H. *Curiosity and exploratory behavior.* New York: Macmillan, 1965.

Frager, S. R., and Stern, C. The use of 5th and 6th graders as tutors of kindergarten children in prereading skills. *Reading Teacher*, 1970, 23, 403–405.

Gartner, A., Kohler, M. C., and Giessman, F. *Children teach children: Learning by teaching.* New York: Harper & Row, 1971.

Gates, A. I. Recitation as a factor in memorizing. *Archives of Psychology*, 1917, 6, No. 40.

Glaser, R. Psychology and instructional technology. In R. Glaser (Ed.), *Training research and education*. Pittsburgh: University of Pittsburgh Press, 1962. Pp. 1–30.

Glass, G. V. Educational knowledge use. *The Educational Forum*, 1971, 36, 21–29.

Gratch, G. Response alternation in children: A developmental study of orientations to uncertainty. *Vita Humana*, 1964, 7, 49–60.

Hunt, J. *Intelligence and experience*. New York: Ronald Press, 1961.

Kagan, J. Reflection-impulsivity: The generality and dynamics of conceptual tempo. *Journal of Abnormal Psychology*, 1966, 71, 71–74.

———, Rosman, B. L., Kay, D., Albert, J., and Phillips, W. Information processing in the child: Significance of analytic and reflective attitudes. *Psychological Monographs*, 1964, 78 (Whole No. 578).

Keislar, E. R. A descriptive approach to classroom motivation. *Journal of Teacher Education*, 1960, XI, 310–315.

———. Teaching children to solve problems: A research goal. *Journal of Research and Development in Education*, 1969, 3, 3–14.

———. Assessment of the four-year-old's preferences for school activities. Paper presented at NCME, February 5, 1971, New York City.

———, and Blumfield, P. A peer tutoring game for four-year-olds. Technical Report. U.C.L.A. Early Childhood Research Center, 1972.

———, and Phinney, J. Young children's use of an information source in self-instruction. *Audio-visual Communications Review*, in press.

———, and McNeil, J. D. Teaching scientific theory to first-grade pupils by auto-instructional device. *Harvard Education Review*, 1961, 31, 73–83.

Kozol, J. Free schools: A time for candor. *Saturday Review*, 1972, 4, 51–54.

Lipe, D., and Jung, S. M. Manipulating incentives to enhance school learning. *Review of Educational Research*, 1971, 41, 249–280.

Logan, F. A. Incentive theory, reinforcement, and education. In R. Glaser (Ed.), *The nature of reinforcement*. New York: Academic Press, 1971. Pp. 45–61.

Markle, S. M. *Good frames and bad: A grammar of frame writing*. New York: John Wiley, 1969.

Munn, N. L. Learning in children. In L. Carmichael (Ed.), *Manual of child psychology*. New York: Wiley, 1954. Pp. 374–458.

Olson, D. *Cognitive development*. New York: Academic Press, 1970.

Platt, J. A revolutionary manifesto. *The Center Magazine*, 1972, 5, 34–52.

Resnick, L. B. Teacher behavior in an informal British infant school. Paper presented at the annual meeting of the American Educational Research Association, New York City, 1971.

Reynolds, L. J. An analysis of self-instructional skills students require for learning within the IPI Mathematics Classroom. Unpublished paper, Learning Research and Development Center, University of Pittsburgh, 1971.

————, and Leinhardt, G. Procedures for the individualized classroom: Trainee's manual. Unpublished paper, Learning Research and Development Center, University of Pittsburgh, 1970.

Rogers, C. R. *Freedom to learn: A view of what education might become.* Columbus, Ohio: Charles E. Merrill, 1969.

Skinner, B. F. *Beyond freedom and dignity.* New York: Knopf, 1971.

Veroff, J. Social comparison and the development of achievement motivation. Charles P. Smith (Ed.), *Achievement-related motives in children.* Russell Sage Foundation, New York, 1969.

Weir, M. W. Developmental changes in problem-solving strategies. *Psychological Review,* 1964, *71,* 473–490.

White, R. W. Motivation reconsidered: The concept of competence. *Psychological Review,* 1959, *66,* 297–333.

# ~«( IV )»~
# NEW DIRECTIONS
# IN SCHOOLING

## ᵒᵛᴼ⟨ 7 ⟩ᴼᵛᵒ

# Educating Females and Males
# to Be Alive and Well
# in Century Twenty-One

### ALBERTA E. SIEGEL

American psychology has been dominated by the study of learning. The processes by which rats, mice, monkeys, and even human beings acquire new behaviors have been carefully studied in literally thousand of experiments in hundreds of psychological laboratories around the land. Our most respected theorists have been our learning theorists. Experiments on learning dominate our textbooks and our lecture courses.

American social thought has been dominated by faith in education. Americans see education as the path to the good life, as a social elevator, as the essential qualifications for a job, as the solution to various social ills. We invest not only our money but also, and more importantly, our time, in a massive educational effort supported by local government, state government, now the federal government, and also by private foundations and trusts.

Given the preoccupation of American psychologists with learning, and the preoccupation of all Americans with education, it is easy for a psychologist to equate learning and education. If something can be learned, then it must be the task of the schools to teach it.

### THE GROWING BURDEN OF EXPECTATIONS
### FOR OUR SCHOOLS

In the last decade much of psychological research has been devoted to demonstrating the importance of early learning. There is now a substantial research literature showing how central the learning is that occurs in the first few years of life. The response of many Americans to these findings has been to extend the educational establishment downward into early childhood. If learning at age four is important, then we'd better have schools for four-year-olds. We are identifying important learning that occurs in the second and third year of life; already we hear suggestions that this means that toddlers should be schooled. And as Americans ponder the new flood of researches on infancy, showing how much is acquired during the very first year of life, there is talk about the mother as a teacher and the crib as a school.

In the nineteenth century, America's social thinkers tended to believe that most behavior was innate. People were competitive because of a competitive instinct. Acquisitiveness was an instinct. So were generosity and nobility. The behavioral differences among individuals were not ignored by these social thinkers; they regarded these differences as innate also. Blacks were thought to be inherently and intrinsically different from whites, and females were thought to be instinctively different from males. Given these stamped-in differences among people, differences which were not based on learning and therefore had nothing to do with education, the task of schools was relatively simple. A few skills were acknowledged to be based on learning and the task of the schools was to concentrate on developing those few skills. Reading and writing must be learned, and thus it was the task of the schools to teach these skills. No one thought that a child would spontaneously come to understand geography and American history. But he could learn to understand them if given the proper instruction.

Throughout the twentieth century, American social thought has come to assert that most behavior is learned. We no longer speak of a competitive instinct: we believe people learn to be competitive. Acquisitiveness is seen to be a learned habit. Even generosity and nobility are thought to be fostered and enhanced by benign learning settings. More, we now see behavorial differences as based on learning. No longer do we see black-white differences as innate and inherent; now we regard them as the product of different learning environments. There are even suggestions that females differ from males not because of instinct but because of learning.

I must pause to note that no serious social thinker believes totally in either genetic endowment or social learning as an explanation for all behavior. All of us recognize, and all of us teach our Psychology 1 students and our Educational Psychology students, that behavior results from an interaction of endowment with experience, that the human being is jointly a product of his biological constitution and his life events.

But the increasing emphasis on learning in the twentieth century has created an awesome set of tasks for the schools. For as soon as Americans find that something is learned, they want the schools to teach it. And they want it taught in the morally correct version. If both competitiveness and cooperativeness are acquired through experience, then we'd better arrange a child's school experiences so he learns the correct balance of competition and cooperation. If children do indeed learn to be generous, then let's start devising ways to teach them this trait in our schools. And if differences between blacks and whites are the result of learning, then it is the task of our schools to teach blacks and whites to be equal.

## LEARNING OUTSIDE OF SCHOOL

By equating schooling with learning, we have come to think of our schools as the site of the solutions for all our social problems. It is this thinking I wish to examine here.

Schools are a relatively recent cultural invention. Some schools for a few privileged young people have existed for centuries. The idea of universal education is a very new idea. Until recently, schools were primarily for males, for freemen, and for the wealthy. This remains true in many parts of the world today. In America, schooling for females began more recently than schooling for males, and it is only even more recently that serious efforts were made to offer schooling for blacks, for Native American Indians, and for other minorities. Now we are seeing the opening up of collegiate education to ethnic minorities. And there are fresh efforts to open up professional education to females, in medical schools, law schools, and business schools. So we are still living through and working through the creation of equal educational opportunities for all Americans.

Schools are new, and universal schooling is even newer. But learning is ancient. Take language, for example. It is evident that children *learn* to speak. French children learn to speak French while their cousins across the channel are learning to speak English. The language a child learns depends on the learning environment in which he lives. But language learning was occurring long before there were schools.

Sherwood Washburn estimates that man has been using a phonetic code for communication for the past 40,000 years. This estimate is based on secular changes in brain size and configuration, as inferred from human fossils. At the time man began to use language, all human beings lived in small nomadic groups which made their living by hunting and gathering. Such societies are almost entirely extinct today, so it is easy for us to forget that 99 percent of the span of human life on this planet has been the era of the hunters and gatherers. Only in the last 1 percent of his time on earth has man had agriculture. And industrialization has occurred in the last tiny fraction of that brief period. The world population was smaller in the past than it is at present, of course, but even so 95 percent of all the humans who have ever lived have been hunters and gatherers. It is worth our thinking about how children learned language in the hunting and gathering group.

Our best guess would be that they learned speech the same way they do now: through observation and imitation of the speech of those they loved. What impelled this learning is the same motivation that underlies speech acquisition in today's toddler: the wish to maintain a close emotional exchange with the adult to whom he is attached. Probably youngsters today learn language more readily than was the case 30,000 or 40,000 years ago, for today's youngsters benefit from thousands of years of natural selection for linguistic capacity. There seems little doubt that selective pressures favored the communicator—he had a better chance to survive to adulthood and to reproduce—and that over the ages the contributors to the gene pool have increasingly been those whose nervous systems were best wired for speech acquisition. By now most human infants are born with the potential to develop a central nervous system that will permit social speech. Only moderately supportive social systems are needed to assure the acquisition of language. That such systems are still needed, however, is evidenced by the tragic histories of children when are reared outside of families, for whom no close bonds form to adults. These children are almost invariably retarded in language skills. Even in the best orphanages—the models devised by dedicated pediatricians and social workers, the orphanages in which infants are well fed, well bathed, healthy, and motorically advanced—speech lags behind the orphans' other skills.

We are talking about a skill—the use of language—which most people link with schooling. An individual who speaks ineffectively is thought to be poorly educated. Cultivated speech is said to mark the literate person. But the most reasonable guess is that this skill is acquired in learning environments outside the school, learning environments which have existed for thousands of years, and learning environments which affect the child during what we call the "*pre*-school" years. Schools simply teach the refinements and sophistications of language: reading and writing.

If the point needed to be made any more vividly, I could mention that some specialists in nonverbal communication estimate that 70 percent of all human communication in face-to-face interaction occurs over extra-lexical channels. Like other primates, human beings convey meaning to one another through posture, gesture, facial expression, and vocal intonation. Infants begin to acquire skills in nonverbal communication very early in life. Their gestures and postures display emotions in the first months of life, and the social smile occurs by two or three months. By the time a child is a year old he has a large repertoire of facial expressions and postures by which he communicates with others around him, and also he is adept at reading the meaning of their postures, gestures, and vocal intonations. There is no doubt that these behaviors are learned. There is no doubt that the learning builds on a biological substrate which goes back into man's history into the millennia before humans had lexical speech. There is no doubt that humans were communicating gesturally before any society had schools. And there is little doubt that skill in nonverbal signalling is essential for social success.

For our present purposes it is important only to note that a child can readily learn to read and write only if he has already mastered speaking, listening, and nonlexical signalling. And he will add the sophisticated language skills to his repertoire most readily if his parents value reading and writing, just as he learned gestural communication, speech, and listening in the context of the emotional exchange with his parents and siblings.

The remarks I've been making about language, both lexical and extra-lexical, could perhaps be made as well about other skills we now know to be learned. The learning begins in the very early years. It occurs in the learning environment which is significant for the child because of his strong emotional bonds with the other persons in that environment. It occurs largely through observation and imitation.

It is the family which is the child's most critical learning environment. We have tended to think that schools are where learning occurs. We have tended to say that if something is learned it is the task of the schools to teach it. In fact, some of the most important learning that humans achieve occurs in homes rather than schools. And if that learning fails to occur the child who enters school at age six is impaired, perhaps irremediably, in his potential for learning the skills that schools must teach. Our options are either to extend schooling institutions downward into infancy, or to strengthen families to continue to serve as primary learning environments.

If children are to grow up to be both alive and well in century twenty-one, it will be because we have managed to keep the family alive and well in century twenty. If we achieve that goal in the latter third of our century, then the children we have reared will have the skills and the motivations to achieve that goal in century twenty-one.

When our ancestors were living as hunters and gatherers, there were no professional educators and educational researchers to discuss how to meet the needs of the coming generation. Education occurred in the context of living, as a byproduct of the work and social life of the community. All institutions shared in the responsibility for socialization of the young. Children learned through observation, imitation, and practice, as well as occasionally through formal instruction. The legends and myths told around the fire conveyed the community's moral insights. Work skills were learned through apprenticeship. Children learned what it means to be male and what it means to be female by observing various males and females in their daily lives. Children learned what it means to be young, to be middle-aged, and to be old by their acquaintance with the youthful and the elderly. Learning occurred because the social institutions functioned to permit children to learn.

## REASSESSING OUR SOCIAL LEARNING ENVIRONMENTS

Our children today are born with the learning capabilities of the children in hunting and gathering societies. They can learn readily through observation and imitation, a fact which has been documented by the researches of Professor Albert Bandura and his students.

What can we learn from the hunting and gathering way of life—which was the life style of 95 percent of our ancestors, the life style in the millennia of human evolution from which we have inherited our genetic capacities and potentialities—which will be helpful with today's young savages?

What we can learn is to question the distinction between educational institutions and other social institutions. And we can learn that most socialization is unintentional, a byproduct of the life of the community. When we acknowledge that the child is socialized by all the institutions in which he has a part, then we may begin to examine all of them for the positive contributions they make to the next generation.

### The TV Learning Environment

Recently I have been involved in this way of thinking about television. The American commercial television enterprise is profoundly committed to the notion that TV exists to entertain and to communicate the news.

As a child psychologist, I am struck by the fact that American children spend more hours watching television than they spend in school. I can't fail to believe that such a pervasive activity has lasting effects on children. The evidence for these effects is coming in, and is becoming increasingly convincing. In the meantime, we have common sense as a guide. It seems only good sense to believe that TV watching must affect children, since they spend much time in front of the tube and do so voluntarily.

What has impressed me is the profound unwillingness of most people to think of TV as a learning experience. This unwillingness was evident in the work of the Surgeon General's Scientific Advisory Committee on Television and Social Behavior. Many Americans are deeply committed to the view that learning is serious, learning occurs in schools, learning is what we elect schools boards to worry about. In contrast, television is fun, television is entertainment, television isn't linked to the schools in any meaningful way, and we don't need to think of the TV set as an instructor with the child as its pupil.

When an anthropologist contemplates the hunting and gathering societies and how they socialized their young, he sees no schools and no school boards. What he sees are learning environments, and youngsters being socialized in these. When he contemplates American life today, can he doubt that TV produces a learning environment for our youngsters? Can he doubt its socializing role?

I believe that our society could benefit if we began thinking of many institutions in terms of their functioning in the socialization of the next generation.

### The Community Learning Environment

The community is a learning environment. The child learns from the people around him, as he meets them in supermarkets and banks, as he visits their apartments and houses, as he encounters them in churches and other organizations. He learns what it means to grow old by observing the elderly in his community. He learns about sickness by watching what happens when people in his community fall ill and need medical attention and nursing care. He learns about infancy not only when he is himself an infant but through observing the infants around him and how they are regarded by adults and other children. He learns about marriage through visiting different families, watching what happens when a couple is divorced, observing the effects of a death on a family. He learns about racism by observing who lives where, in what kinds of homes, and by observing who works in what kinds of jobs.

I haven't served on a Surgeon General's Committee for the real estate activity in our country, as I have served on a Surgeon General's Committee to study television. But I think it is a fair guess that the real estate operators are even less aware of their role as educators than the television people are. Most television writers and producers have a dim awareness that there are children watching, though they don't think about children very much and they don't know much about children's thought processes. But are real estate operators thinking about children at all as they develop our new neighborhoods and rearrange older ones? How are they altering the community as a learning environment when they develop separate living facilities for the aged? When retirement communities are built away from cities and towns, we not only change the tax base for our schools, we also change the experience base for our children. No longer will the child confront the realities of aging in his daily life. No longer will he have casual everyday opportunities to know a grandfatherly or grandmotherly older person who loves him in the especially clearsighted and indulgent way that older people love the very young.

I selected this example, rather than the more obvious one of ethnic segregation in housing, just because I think it is slightly less obvious. We all know that it is housing patterns that have segregated our communities. The fact that schools are asked to adjust their arrangements in order to compensate for the inequities perpetrated by another social institution—

the building and real estate industries—is just an example of my general point that Americans ask schools to bear most of the burdens of educating our young while ignoring the educative functions of other social institutions.

## DIRECT AND INDIRECT EFFECTS OF SOCIAL ENVIRONMENTS ON CHILDREN

My general point is that a modern understanding of the psychology of learning compels us to examine all our social institutions as learning environments. And a modern understanding of the central importance of the family in the child's learning compels us to examine all our social institutions to see ways in which they support and strengthen the family, or ways they may compete with it and inadvertently be destructive to the family.

It is naive and arrogant to say that if something is learned then the schools must teach it. Language is but one example of many a skill which is learned outside of school. Realistically, we must examine every social institution to see the contributions it can make to the child's learning. These contributions will be of two kinds: the direct contributions, made through serving as a learning environment for children, and the indirect contributions, made through support to the family.

For example, television makes direct contributions to children's learning by providing them with imagery about social roles, by providing models of language use, by displaying examples of human conflict and how it is resolved, by vaunting certain products that children are urged to use in order to grow big, strong, and powerful, and so forth. Television is indirectly involved in the welfare of children by all that it does bearing on families. In some nations, this fact is recognized in the practice of shutting down the TV transmitters during the dinner period: TV does not compete with parents for the child's attention at the traditional time of family togetherness. Television could be helpful to children if the magnificent teaching potential of the medium were used to teach mothers about mothering. This electronic teacher that brings an integrated message to eye and ear, and that reaches into 96 percent of the homes of this nation, could be a powerful aid to the pediatrician and the nurse in showing mothers how to nurse their babies, how to guard their health, how to encourage social communication early in life, and so forth.

Similarly, the housing industry makes direct contributions to children's learning by creating environments in which children can or cannot meet people at all stages in the life cycle, can or cannot observe people at work, can or cannot easily meet one another to play together, can or cannot explore their neighborhoods without being exposed to mutilation by automobiles. At the same time, it makes indirect contributions to children's lives by the ways it affects families. The housing industry helps to determine how long the daily commute run is for men, and thus how many waking hours a child will spend in the company of his father. The housing industry helps to determine whether a family has privacy, whether family recreation is accessible, and so forth.

## THE SCHOOL AS A SOCIALIZING INSTITUTION

Now so far I doubt that I've written much with which most educators would disagree. Most educators are likely to appreciate the significance of early learning, to recognize the importance of the family to the child, to agree that all social institutions have effects on children, and that we could serve children's welfare by examining these effects.

But now I want to turn this argument back on the schools. For schools are themselves learning environments, and they are also social institutions that can aid the family or can contribute to its further deterioration. We have asked what the television industry is doing to create favorable learning environments for children and adolescents, and what its practices are doing to strengthen families. We may ask the same question of the education establishment.

### Support of the Family

Since schools are set up to educate children, it may seem foolish to ask what schools are doing to enhance learning opportunities for children. But I want to ask that question not about classroom practices but about schools as a social institution. Like every other social institution, the school constitutes a learning environment for children, and thus may affect them directly, and it has effects on the family, which may be either supportive or competing.

An example of the ways schools affect families is the relation of schools to geographical mobility of families. In my opinion, geographical moves have the potential of being destructive to family life. It is because of the dispersal of our population all over the landscape that children now grow up in homes with only two adult relatives (at most) who care about them, far distant from their grandparents and aunts and uncles who might otherwise enrich and diversify their lives and might relieve and aid their parents in time of sickness and family stress. It is the middle class in this country which is geographically mobile, as the businessman father climbs the executive ladder in a major corporation by locating and relocating at various branch offices, or as the academician father moves from one university to another to climb the academic ladder from instructor to professor.

What can schools do about geographical mobility? Here it is important to think of the school as an employer rather than as a classroom. Can schools arrange their employment practices so that it is not necessary for their employees to relocate in order to advance? Can they give the most careful consideration of the qualifications of their own employees before going outside to fill leadership positions? Can they arrange instructional opportunities in their own communities so school employees need not travel in order to advance their own educations? As employers, schools are in a position to be either helpful or destructive to the family lives of their own employees, and in this way to contribute importantly to those we want to be alive and well in century twenty-one.

A second example has to do with the health of the family. Our nation is in a crisis of medical care. We tend to think of schools as contributing to the solution of this problem through schooling: by guiding more young-sters into the health professions, by encouraging students to consider careers in nursing, medical social work, dietetics, physical therapy, rehabilitation, and the like. And we tend to think of the need to establish curricula in these fields in our high schools and junior colleges, as well as in our colleges and universities.

But the schools are also health insurers. The educational establishment constitutes one of the largest networks of employers in the United States. What kind of health care arrangements do schools offer for employees? As an enlightened institution, a school system can be a model health insurer, insisting that school employees are covered for preventive medicine as well as for treatment of illness, insisting that psychiatric coverage is assured as well as coverage for other illnesses, insisting that the employee's family receives the same thorough medical protection that is given to the em-ployee personally. I mention this example not to get off on to the subject of medical care but to provide a common-sense example of a supportive role the schools can play to aid family life.

### Socialization of the Sexes

My remaining examples will have to do with the changing roles of females and males. There has been a lot of talk about ways that schools may participate in the current revolution in women's roles. I'd like to focus my concern on what the schools can do as socializing institutions and as institutions which support family life.

The industrial revolution and subsequent technological revolutions have profoundly altered the lives of males. Because man's work is increasingly mechanized, brain power and personality attributes are increasingly re-placing muscle power as the contribution the individual man makes in his work. This means increasingly lengthy and specialized education for men.

And whereas in the hunting and gathering eras and in the agricultural era, men worked out of their homes, now men's work occurs in factories and offices sometimes far distant from their homes. For today's urban and suburban male, the home is the place where he sleeps at night, where he performs brief morning ablutions and takes a hasty breakfast, and where he spends his evenings for a few brief hours of family life.

The effects of the industrial revolution have been felt by women much more recently. They include a change in the ways food and clothing are manufactured and processed, and thus a change in the work that must be done within the home. They also include an increasing emphasis on a money economy, with the result that many women need to earn money to meet their families' needs. Also significant are twentieth-century advances in contraception and in medical care of mothers and children, with the result that women can plan their families, few of them die in childbirth, and few of their children die. All of this is new, and so is the modern emphasis on a small family. A woman's life expectation today is 20 years longer than it was in 1900. These changes in women's lives come together in the increased employment of women outside the home. Only in this generation are the majority of adult women likely to be working outside the home, but the proportion of women in the working force has been increasing steadily throughout the century and is likely to continue to increase as we inch towards century twenty-one.

How should schools respond to these radical changes in the lives of women? The tendency has been to make direct responses: to alter the curriculum and rewrite the textbooks. This is all to the good. Certainly it is appropriate to launch guidance programs for women to encourage them to enter careers in science, law, medicine, and engineering, as well as in librarianship, nursing, teaching, and social work. Certainly we do need a revolution in admissions policies at the level of higher education, to enable young women to synchronize their education with their personal and family lives. We must find ways to enable a college woman to transfer from one institution to another when she marries and her husband relocates. We must find ways to offer a college education to women with families, enabling them to come to college on a part-time basis and at hours suited to family life. All of this is so obvious it is easy to overlook the fact that many institutions of higher education have hardly started to make these changes. Among other direct responses, probably it is worthwhile to scrutinize our children's readers, to see whether Jane is destined to be a homebound drudge and Dick is on his way to growing up as a male chauvinist. And certainly it is important to expand the horizons of our history books, to see that children learn more about our past than the political history of white males.

But my guess is that the most important and significant responses are going to be the indirect ones. And this is my point of distinction between education and learning. It is not as educational institutions but as environments for learning and as social institutions that our schools are likely to have their greatest usefulness in enabling individuals to adapt to the changing roles of men and women. Indeed, most of the direct responses have already been made: more than any other social institution in our society, our schools have created opportunities for females to develop their abilities. It is precisely because we have so many well-educated women that we are impressed by the barriers to them in science, medicine, and law. It is precisely because our schools have already shown how capable girls are of achievement that we wonder why they have no more opportunities for using their talents in business, finance, higher education, politics, and so on.

What can we do to create schools which are environments for learning and are social institutions that promote family strength and that aid males and females in adapting to the requirements of century twenty-one? I have already mentioned policies which reduce the pressures to geographical mobility and thus aid the extended family to stay together. And I have mentioned policies which enhance the medical and psychiatric services to families with a member who is employed by the schools. A third contribution schools can make is to avoid sex-role stereotyping in employment.

If children learn through observation, as I believe our research shows they do, then our children are going to learn about sex roles by observing what kinds of jobs are held by males and females in the institutions which are open to them. Children will learn about sex-role stereotypes in our churches, by watching TV, in our banks and supermarkets. They will also learn in our schools Who are the secretaries? Who are the custodians? Who are the shop teachers? Who are the nurses? Who are the principals? Who are the kindergarten teachers? Who are the librarians? As an employing institution, our schools can serve to reduce sex-role stereotyping by giving children the opportunity to meet physicians who are females and librarians who are males, the opportunity to take classes from female science teachers and male chefs.

Here I am suggesting that we put our money where our mouth is. All the high school guidance lectures and pamphlets about women in science are not going to have the effect of knowing one woman scientist who is happy and effective in her work. All the talk in the world about career opportunities for women in engineering is as nothing compared to the opportunity to meet and work with one woman who is a contributing engineer.

A fourth suggestion is based on the observation that people marry people similar to themselves. A psychologist often marries another psychologist, a lawyer is likely to marry another lawyer, and a teacher is very probably going to marry another teacher. How can our schools as social institutions contribute to family stability and family strength when both parents are in the same profession? As employers they can minimize the barriers to the employment of spouses.

Schools should reexamine their nepotism policies for their costs and benefits. We have all been preoccupied with the dangers in employing both a woman and her husband. We fear bloc voting. We fear favoritism in promotions. We fear jealousy of the family earning two salaries. In this preoccupation, we have failed to consider the dangers in not employing both a woman and her husband. We have ignored the strains on a marriage when the two partners have to commute some distance in order to serve in independent institutions. We have ignored the even more profound strains when one partner is unable to use the education he or she has received and when that partner sees the marriage as blocking his or her professional growth. And we have also ignored the benefits of employing both a wife and her husband. When a couple are both teachers in the same school, the students in that school have the opportunity to observe a marriage relation which includes intellectual respect. They have the opportunity to learn to know a woman who is both a wife and a professional person and to observe that she fulfills both roles effectively. They also have the opportunity to observe the strains that some women experience in combining marriage with professional work, and thus to learn that this challenge is not for every woman. When both a wife and a husband are employed in the same institution, that institution becomes a richer learning environment for the youngsters being socialized in it. And that institution is contributing to family stability by providing an opportunity for a marriage between professionals to work comfortably. These are very real benefits, and we ought to consider these benefits in our cost-benefits reanalysis of nepotism. In my view there's nothing wrong with nepotism as long as you keep it in the family.

My fifth suggestion comes from everyone who has made a serious study of women in our current era. Part-time jobs are the way society can use women's educational achievements today while not interfering with women's work as wives and mothers. Our schools should be especially sensitive to this need. Schools are concerned with children, and it is folly for them to be engaged in employment practices which interfere with a woman's ability to be a fine mother to her children. The part-time job permits a woman to achieve independently in the world of work while continuing to give her children and her husband the attention and care they require from her. As employers, schools can be pioneers in creating more and more part-time positions for women. Especially valuable would be jobs whose hours coincide with the hours children are in school, so that employed mothers may be at home when their children are. Needless to say, I am urging part-time jobs not only for teachers, administrators, and other professional staff but also for service employees, clerical workers.

With part-time jobs available, the schools will become interesting learning environments in which the male and female students may observe both women and men in a variety of work activities. Their acquaintance with women workers will not be limited to older women whose children have grown nor to the very young women who have not yet had children, but rather they will become acquainted with women from all stages of life and thus will be enriched in their understanding of what it means to be a woman in an industrial era.

## SUMMARY

How can we educate our children to be alive and well in century twenty-one? To begin with, we must recognize that their learning equipment is the result of evolutionary selection within the context of hunting and gathering society. They learn from all their experiences, not just from those labeled "education," and they learn through observation, imitation, and practice. This means we must examine all our social institutions as learning environments for youngsters. Second, we must recognize that the most important learning occurs within the family, from the people with whom the child has strong emotional bonds. Other social institutions can aid children to be alive and well in century twenty-one by aiding the family. This means examining our social institutions for the unintended consequences that technological advances may have had for the family. Is there a sort of pollution of the family caused by industrialization, electronic communication, geographical dispersal, and the other marvels of the twentieth century? Schools can set an example for all social institutions by examining not only the direct educative influences they have on children but also the indirect ones. Females and males will be more likely to be alive and well in century twenty-one if our schools reform all aspects of the learning environment they provide for children, and if they modify all their practices to bring them into line with the continuing viability and strength of the family.

## ⌁ 8 ⌁

# How Do the Young
# Become Adults?

### JAMES S. COLEMAN

It is important to ask, along with specific questions about how schools function, more general questions about the development from childhood through youth to adulthood. Only by continuing to ask these more general questions can we avoid waking up some day to find that educational institutions are finely tuned and efficiently designed to cope with the problems of an earlier day. Among the more general questions, we need to ask how it is that the young become adults, and what are the current and changing roles of various formal institutions in that development.

There are three formal institutions that are especially important in examining the changes that are occurring in the way youth are brought to adulthood. One is the school, another is the family, and a third is the workplace. I will reserve the school till last, because changes in the other two institutions proceed from other causes, without regard for their consequences for the young, while schools are explicitly designed with consequences for the young as their primary goal. Thus the family and the workplace—together with certain other aspects of society—form the environment within which the school functions.

## CHANGES IN THE FAMILY

It is necessary only to give a quick overview of changes in the family's function in bringing children to adulthood, because those changes have been so great, and need only to be brought to attention. Classically, the family was the chief educational institution for the child, because he carried out most of his activities within it until he left it to form his own. That juncture in life was his transition to adult status—the transition to economic self-sufficiency and family head. The timing of this transition differed widely from place to place and from one economic setting to another. On an Irish farm, it may have been age 35 or even older. In an industrial city, it may have been 16 or even younger. But the transition to full adulthood has characteristically taken place when the former child married and either formed a new household or formed a sub-household within his parental family.

The family has gone through two major transitions that sharply limit its occupational training of the young. The first of these occurred when the father went out to work, into a shop or an office, and thus began to carry out his major productive activities away from home behind the closed doors of an organization. The second occurred when the mother went out to work or otherwise stopped carrying out her major productive activities in the home. Before the first transition, families contained the major productive activities of society. Thus the young learned not only the whole variety of things that one commonly associates with the family, they also learned their principal occupational skills and functions—if not in the family, then structurally close to it, in an apprentice relation.

For boys, this occupational learning within the family began to vanish as the father went out to work in a shop or an office. For girls, it continued longer, learning household work, cooking, sewing, child care from the mother, whose principal occupation that was. But by now in most families that second transition has taken place as well: the mother's principal occupation is no longer household work, for that work now occupies little of her time and attention. Either she goes out to work like her husband, or occupies herself in other activities which do not require the aid of her daughters. Even child care is minimal, as family sizes have declined. As an economist recently stated, "The home closes down during the day."

Thus the family as a source of occupational learning has declined as it lost its place as the central productive institution of society. But as both adults have come to carry out their central activities outside the home, they have removed other functions from the home and family as well. Friends are drawn from occupation, and adult cocktail parties have replaced neighborhood or extended family gatherings in the social life of the husband and wife. Less and less does the husband's and wife's social life take place in a setting that includes children. Some leisure activities are still carried out as a family, so I don't intend to overstate the case. But the point is that as these large occupational activities of adults moved out of the home, they took others with them, leaving it a less rich place in opportunities for learning for its younger members.

## CHANGES IN THE WORKPLACE

Changes in the workplace, subsequent to its removal from the home into specialized economic institutions, have also affected the movement of the young into adulthood. The major changes have been away from small organizations to large ones; away from ad hoc informal hiring practices to formal procedures with formal credentials required of applicants; away from using children in secondary and service activities toward excluding them from workplaces under the guise of "protection"; away from jobs requiring low educational credentials toward jobs requiring more education; away from loosely organized occupational settings in which workers participated with varying schedules and varying amounts of time toward a rigidly-defined "full-time job" with a fixed schedule and fixed time commitment.

All of these trends (apart from some very minor and very recent movements in the other direction in a few of these dimensions) have led the workplace to become less available and less useful to the young until they enter it as full-time workers at the end of a longer and longer period of full-time schooling.[1]

These changes in the family and in occupational institutions have led both to become less useful as settings where the young can learn. In the family, the young remain, while the activities from which they could learn have moved out; in workplaces, the activities from which the young could learn remain, but the young themselves have been excluded. This exclusion places youth more on the fringes of society, outside its important institutions. If one is young, it is difficult to get a loan, to buy on credit, to rent an apartment, to have one's signature accepted for any of the many things that are commonplace for adults. The reason is simple: the young have no institutional base, they are a lumpen proletariat outside those institutions of society that are recognized by other institutions and give legitimacy to those persons who are within them.

Before turning to changes in the school, it is important to note one central aspect of the learning that occurred in home and workplaces, and still occurs,

---

[1] There are some complications to these trends, and some statistics which appear to go in the opposite direction. For example, the labor force participation rates for persons aged 16 to 21 enrolled in school increased between 1960 and 1970, from 35 to 40 percent for men and 25 to 36 percent for women. But this change reflects an increase in school-going by those who in 1960 would have been only working. The proportion of persons aged 16 to 21 enrolled in school was much higher in 1970 than in 1960. This increase was largely due to a lack of full-time jobs in the labor force for a greatly expanded age cohort. Thus for many, education became the full-time activity, and labor force participation was restricted to part-time or in-and-out work.

though to a sharply reduced extent. It is learning which is variously called "incidental learning" or "experiential learning." It is learning by acting and experiencing the consequences of that action. It is learning through occupying a role with responsibility for actions that affect others. It is learning that is recognized in colloquial parlance as taking place in "the school of hard knocks." It is not learning that proceeds in the way that learning typically takes place in the classroom, where the first step is cognitive understanding, and the last step—often omitted—is acting on that understanding.

## CHANGES IN THE SCHOOL

When the major educational functions were in the home, the school was an auxiliary and supplementary institution with two functions. First, for the small fraction of the population whose occupational destination was clerical or academic, it taught a large portion of the occupational skills: languages, mathematics, philosophy, history. Second, for the large majority, it taught the basic skills of literacy and numeracy: reading, writing, and arithmetic. Then, as the changes in family and workplace took place, the school began to take on two additional functions: first, to provide occupational training for the increasing fraction of occupations that seemed to require technical book learning (occupations ranging from engineering to journalism); and second, to perform some of the educational activities that were not occupational, but had been carried out to differing degrees and often with indifferent success in the family, ranging from music appreciation to civics. In addition to these explicit and positive functions, the school began to carry out an important but largely passive function as well: to house the young while the parents were off in their specialized adult activities outside the home. This is the function often derogatorily described as the "baby-sitting" function of the school. As women come more and more into the labor force, and desire to participate even more than they do, the demand for such baby-sitting agencies has increased, extending downward in age to day-care centers for the very young. And as occupational opportunities for the young have lessened, the baby-sitting function has extended upward in age, with the universities, colleges, junior colleges, and community colleges acting as temporary holding stations on the way to adulthood.

This transformation of the schools in response to society has had a consequence that is important in considering the path to becoming adult. This is the massive enlargement of the *student* role of young persons, to fill the vacuum that the changes in the family and workplace created. The student role of young persons has become enlarged to the point where that role constitutes the major portion of their youth. But the student role is not a role of taking action and experiencing consequences. It is not a role in which one learns by hard knocks. It is a relatively passive role, always in preparation for action, but never acting. In attempting to provide the learning that had earlier taken place through experiential learning in the home and at the workplace, the school kept the same classroom mode of learning that was its hallmark: it not only moved the setting of those learning activities from outside the school to within; it changed the method from learning through experience as a responsible actor to learning through being taught as a student. There are some exceptions but the general pattern followed that of the classical school, in which a *teacher* was the medium through which learning was expected to take place. This replaced *action* as the medium through which learning had taken place in the family or the workplace. The student role, in which a person waits to be taught, became central to the young person's life.

The consequence of the expansion of the student role, and the action-poverty it implies for the young, has been an increased restiveness among the young. They are shielded from responsibility, and they become irresponsible; they are held in a dependent status, and they come to act as dependents; they are kept away from productive work, and they become unproductive. But even if we saw no signs of irresponsibility, stagnant dependency, and lack of productivity, the point would remain the same: the school, when it has tried to teach nonintellective things, does so in the only way it knows how, the way designed to teach intellective capabilities: through a teacher, transmitting cognitive skills and knowledge, in a classroom, to students.

## SCHOOLING VS. EDUCATION

Although the complex problems created by these changes cannot be solved easily, I believe it would be a step toward a solution if we began to conceive of matters a little differently. In particular, the problems become clearer if we wipe away the confusion between "schooling" and "education." Previously, it was natural that schooling could have been confused with education —for schooling was that part of the education of the young which took place formally, and thus had to be planned for and consciously provided. But the larger part of education took place outside the school. The child spent most of his time outside the school; school was a small portion of his existence. It taught him to read and write and work with numbers, but the most important parts of education it did not provide: learning about work, both the skills and the habits, learning how to function in society, learning how to be a father or mother, husband or wife, learning to take care of others and to take responsibility for others. Because these things were learned informally, through experience, or at least without formal organization, they could be disregarded, and "education" could come to be identified with "schooling."

But much of this other education evaporates as work takes place behind closed doors and as the family is reduced as a locus of important activities. "Schooling" meanwhile continues to mean much the same thing that it did before, except extended in time: the learning of intellectual skills. Thus although schooling remains a small portion of education, it occupies an increasingly larger portion of a young person's time, while the remaining portion of his education is *not* well provided by ordinary, everyday, unplanned activities. Consequently, if an appropriate reform of education is to be made, it must begin with this fact: schooling is not all of education, and the other parts of education require just as much explicit planning and organization as does schooling.

Once this is recognized, then the way is paved for creation of a true educational system—not merely a system of schools, but a system of education that covers nonintellectual learning as well. If one were to go too quickly to a possible solution, or pattern for the future, he would see this as immediately leading toward a multi-track school system in which some young people concentrate on intellectual skills while others concentrate on "practical" or "mechanical" or "vocational" skills. But this pattern fails to recognize clearly the impact of the preceding separation of schooling and education: it is not only *some* young people who need the nonintellective portions of education, it is all. Thus it is not the *persons* who must be divided into different tracks to learn different skills; it is the *time* of *each* person that must be so divided. Further, the division is not merely a division between intellectual skills and vocational or practical skills. It is a division among a variety of skills, only some of which are intellectual or vocational. If I were asked to catalog the skills that should be learned in the educational system before age eighteen, I would certainly include all these:

1. Intellectual skills, the kinds of things that schooling at its best teaches.
2. Skills of some occupation that may be filled by a secondary school graduate, so that every eighteen-year-old would be accredited in some occupation, whether he continued in school or not.
3. Decision-making skills: that is, those skills of making decisions in complex situations where consequences follow from the decisions.
4. General physical and mechanical skills: skills allowing the young person to deal with physical and mechanical problems he will confront outside work, in the home or elsewhere.
5. Bureaucratic and organizational skills: how to cope with a bureau-

cratic organization, as an employee or a customer or a client, or a manager or an entrepreneur.

6. Skills in the care of dependent persons: skill in caring for children, old persons, and sick persons.
7. Emergency skills: how to act in an emergency, or an unfamiliar situation, in sufficient time to deal with the emergency.
8. Verbal communication skills in argumentation and debate.

This catalog of skills is certainly not all-inclusive, nor are all the skills listed on the same level of generality. They do, however, give a sense of the scope of what I believe must be explicitly included in education.

## THE ORGANIZATION OF EDUCATION

The next question becomes, "How is this all to be organized?" Or perhaps, "How do we change the schools to do all this?" But the second question puts the matter wrong. My principal point, and it is the central point of the educational pattern of the future that I envision, is that we do *not* attempt to have the schools do all this. Schools are prepared to do what they have done all along: teach young people intellectual things, both by giving them information and giving them intellectual tools, such as literacy, mathematics, and foreign languages. Schools are not prepared to teach these other skills—and the history of their attempts to change themselves so that they could do this shows only one thing: that these other activities—whether they are vocational education, driver training, consumer education, civics, home economics, or something else—have always played a secondary and subordinate role in schools, always in the shadow of academic performance. The mode of organization of schools, the fact that they are staffed by teachers who themselves have been measured by academic performance, the fact that they lead in a natural progression to more and more intellectually specialized institutions, the universities and then graduate schools—all this means that they are destined to fail as educational institutions in areas other than teaching of intellectual skills.

The pattern for the future, then, as I see it, is one in which the school comes to be reduced in importance and scope and time in the life of a young person from age twelve onward, with the explicit recognition that it is providing only a portion of education. This reduction would necessarily occur, because these other skills must be learned as well—many of them by experience and practice, some of them including a little admixture of teaching.

It then becomes necessary to ask just where these other skills would be learned. An immediate response, and an incorrect one, I believe, would be to attempt to design specialized institutions to teach these things, as vocational schools were designed to teach occupational skills—incorrect because if my arguments are correct, then these activities are best learned not by being taught but by acting. Thus it is necessary to ask where the action is. The answer is clear: it is in those specialized economic institutions of society into which first men, then women, went out from the family to work. It is in the occupational institutions of society. Women have learned this through the social-psychological poverty of home and neighborhood and have deserted the home for these workplaces.

Thus this education can appropriately take place only in the economic institutions of society—those organizations behind whose door adults vanish while the child vanishes inside the walls of the school. Such education could not be hit-or-miss, merely placing a young person on the job or in an apprentice situation. It would be necessary to carefully lay out the skills that were necessary to learn, more carefully than I have done in the catalog of eight skills I've listed, and to organize the young person's experiences in such a way that he learns these skills. This would involve, of course, more than one institution outside the school. And it would require brilliance both in conception and in execution if it is to work well in early days. For it involves nothing less than a breaking open of the economic institutions of society, from factories to hospitals, a removing of the insulation that separates them from the young, and giving them an explicit role in the education of the young. How this would be done will differ from society to society: in the free enterprise capitalist economy of the United States, it could probably best begin by providing the young with entitlements that could be redeemed by businesses and other enterprises that try to provide the appropriate learning experiences. In other countries, it might better be done in another way. But the end result would be similar—the young would be integrated into the economic activities of society from a very early age, *without* stopping their schooling, but merely by stopping the dilution of schooling that has occurred in recent years. The economic organizations of society would necessarily change, and change radically, to incorporate the young—not to become schools, but to become institutions in which work is designed not only for productive efficiency, but for learning efficiency as well. The revolution necessary in society is, if I am correct, a revolution within these occupational institutions—from General Motors to government agencies—from business offices to airports.

A reorganization of education in this way would require, if it is to be effective, standards of performance and criteria to be met in the areas other than intellectual, so that the credentials of a young person would be far broader than those implied by the various diplomas and degrees that have been carried over in modified form from an early period. Some of the credentials would be based on performance tests such as those used in industries and skilled crafts today. Others would be based on performance ratings by supervisors and on letters of recommendation. For developing other criteria, inventiveness and imagination would be necessary. But the essential point is that those skills must be just as explicitly evaluated and form just as much a portion of a young person's credentials as intellectual skills do today.

## IMPLICATIONS OF REORGANIZING EDUCATION

There are a number of important implications to this reorganization of the path toward adulthood. If we recognize that it requires an explicit breaking open of work organizations to incorporate the young, the most direct implication is an enormous transformation of these economic institutions. Their product would be not only goods and services to be marketed, but also learning, the latter paid from public funds as schools are today. They would become much more diversified institutions, no longer preserving the fiction that nothing but production occurs within them, but recognizing that much of adults' social lives, and most of their time expenditures, takes place within them, and expanding that recognition into explicit design of this experience.

A less direct implication of this reorganization of education is that it would reduce the relationship between educational performance and family educational background or social class. In schools, the pervasive power of testing on intellectual criteria—the only real criteria the school knows—exacerbates and emphasizes the inequalities of academic background that children bring with them to school. If education is appropriately defined to include these other equally important skills, then the artificially-heightened disparity between students from "advantaged" and "disadvantaged" backgrounds will be reduced—but only, of course, if these other activities are carried out in their natural habitat, rather than in the school, which constitutes an uncongenial setting for them.

Finally, a still less direct implication of this reorganization of education is related to the current controversy about school integration through balancing of the races or social classes in school. That controversy, which reflects a real problem where residential segregation is pronounced—as it is in all large urban areas—cannot be solved as long as education is identified with a school building containing classrooms and teachers. It can be solved if formal education takes place largely outside the schools and in economic institutions—for it is the economic institutions that of all those in society are the least segregated by race and in which racial integration produces least friction—because it occurs in a setting with work to be done in an organized, rather than anarchic, structure of interpersonal relations.

This effect of such a reorganized system of education in integrating the society racially is not an accidental one. It arises because this reorganization is not an ad hoc, makeshift patching up of outworn institutions. It is a reorganization that recognizes fundamental structural changes in society—the drying up of family functions and the specialization of economic activities— and asks where in such an emerging social structure is the appropriate locus for the young, if they are to have the opportunity for moving to adulthood. The answer is that the young belong where everyone else is, and where the action is: inside the economic institutions where the productive activities of society take place.

# Name Index

# Subject Index